ECONOMISTS FOR BEGINNERS

Published by Writers and Readers Publishing Cooperative Society Ltd. 1982
Reprinted 1982

Text and illustrations © 1982 Bernard Canavan

Printed at the University Press, Oxford

Cased ISBN 0 906495 51 2
Paper ISBN 0 906495 52 0

Seven Economists in their own Words

Here are seven economic theories of value, production and distribution. Each provides an account of capital accumulation and the claims of different social classes for a share of the wealth created. Each economist explains the concepts in his own words, edited and indicated by italic print. Quotes are drawn from a single volume of the writer's work in the case of Smith*, Malthus, Mill, Marshall and Keynes. Ricardo and Marx developed their theories over several volumes and quotations reflect these sources.

* Glossary and biographies can be consulted at the back of this book.

4

Economics is not a new subject. Discussions on value and distribution can be found in the works of the Greeks; but it first attained the position of an independent science in the latter half of the 18th century. Among the pioneers in this field were the English writer, William Petty, who published his **Political Arithmetick** in 1690; the Irish banker, James Cantillion, whose **Essay on the Nature of Commerce in General** appeared in 1755; and James Stuart, the Scottish writer, who brought out his **Principles of Political Economy** in 1767.

HEARD THE ONE ABOUT THE ENGLISHMAN, THE IRISHMAN AND THE SCOTSMAN?

Sorry to upset your little joke, but we French have something to say too.
I'm François Quesnay.
I and my colleagues in Paris were known as Physiocrats. In my own work, **Tableau Economique**, published in 1758, I traced the distribution of wealth among the various social classes over the course of a year – I maintained that only agriculture produced social wealth...I think that's where I went wrong.

6

Why was there this great interest in the production of wealth about this time?

I SHOULD HAVE THOUGHT THAT WAS OBVIOUS — THE DEVELOPMENT OF CAPITALISM.

YES, BUT WHY DID CAPITALISM DEVELOP ... THEN?

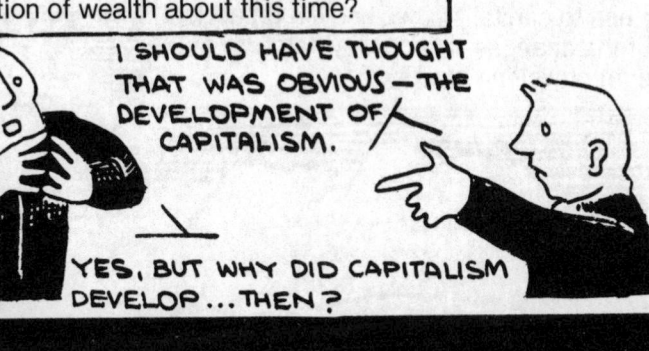

To this question there has been a variety of answers.

ON MY RIGHT, MAX WEBER ANALYSED THE CHANGES IN THE SPIRITUAL ATTITUDE TOWARDS WEALTH.

ON MY LEFT, KARL MARX, SAW CAPITALISM DEVELOP AS A RESULT OF CHANGES IN PRODUCTION AND CLASS STRUGGLE.

And the debate goes on...

But if we are uncertain of the forces that gave rise to capitalism, we know a great deal about the changes this new system wrought on British society.

In 1760 the population was estimated to be about 8m., by the first census in 1851 it had reached 21m. with the major portion concentrated in the new towns. In 1750 there were only two towns in Britain with over 50,000: by 1850 there were twenty-nine.

Supplies to these new centres demanded better communications. Between 1750 and 1790 there were 1,600 Acts of Parliament passed to improve the 24,000 miles of turnpike roads. And by the turn of the century nearly 3,000 miles of canals had been completed.

Industrial production proceeded apace. Output of coal rose from 3m. tons in 1750 to nearly 50m. in 1850; iron production from an estimated 20,000 to 2m. tons and cotton from 8,000 to 300,000 tons during the same period.

This growth in production generated increased national income. Estimates of national income (at current prices) put it at about £230m. in 1800, in 1830 £350m. and in 1850 £525m. with national income per head doubling from about £12 to £24 per annum.

Water-power and muscle-power provided the impetus for this growth in wealth, but it was soon supplemented by steam-power. In 1783 the first of the new rotative steam engines was built by the engineers Boulton and Watt, and by the time their patent ran out in 1800, they had built 500.

It was only a short step from harnessing an engine to a pump or hammer to harnessing it to a carriage — and with that, the age of the railway began. This provided an insatiable demand for steel, coal and British goods on a world-wide scale.

What effect did these developments have on British social structure from Adam Smith to Keynes, and what were the ideas which dominated social policy during these two centuries?

John Locke 1632-1704
Natural Law

' Society is natural and best when left alone. '

Jeremy Bentham 1748-1832
Utilitarianism

' Society should be governed by the principle of the greatest happiness for the greatest number. '

Herbert Spencer 1820-1903
Social Darwinism

' Society is made up of social organisms subject to the survival of the fittest. '

Karl Marx 1818-1883
Class War

' Society is made up of classes in perpetual struggle. '

10

PERCENTAGE OF TOTAL FAMILIES

NOBILITY.

PROFESSIONS, GOVERNMENT SERVICE

AGRICULTURE

GENERAL LABOUR

MANUFACTURE

TRADE DISTRIBUTION

UPPER CLASS

UPPER MIDDLE CLASS

MIDDLE CLASS

LOWER MIDDLE CLASS

SKILLED LABOUR

LESS SKILLED LABOUR

AGRICULTURE AND UNSKILLED LABOUR

UPPER AND MIDDLE CLASS

LOWER MIDDLE CLASS

SKILLED LABOUR

SEMI- AND UNSKILLED LABOUR

UPPER CLASS

MIDDLE CLASS

LOWER MIDDLE CLASS

SKILLED LABOUR

SEMI-SKILLED

UNSKILLED

11

And how did economists fit into all this professionally and intellectually?

We entered economics from a variety of different starting points. Smith, Mill and Marx were all philosophers first; Malthus, Marshall and Keynes all studied maths at university, and Ricardo was an amateur scientist before he took up economics.

Ricardo made his fortune on the stock market and retired to study. Mill was an administrator all his life, and Marx made a precarious living as a journalist with a little help from his friend Friedrich Engels.

All of us have strong political and moral views. Mill and Ricardo were Members of Parliament; Marx organised the first working men's international, and Keynes was an advisor to the government.

1

Adam Smith
1723   1790

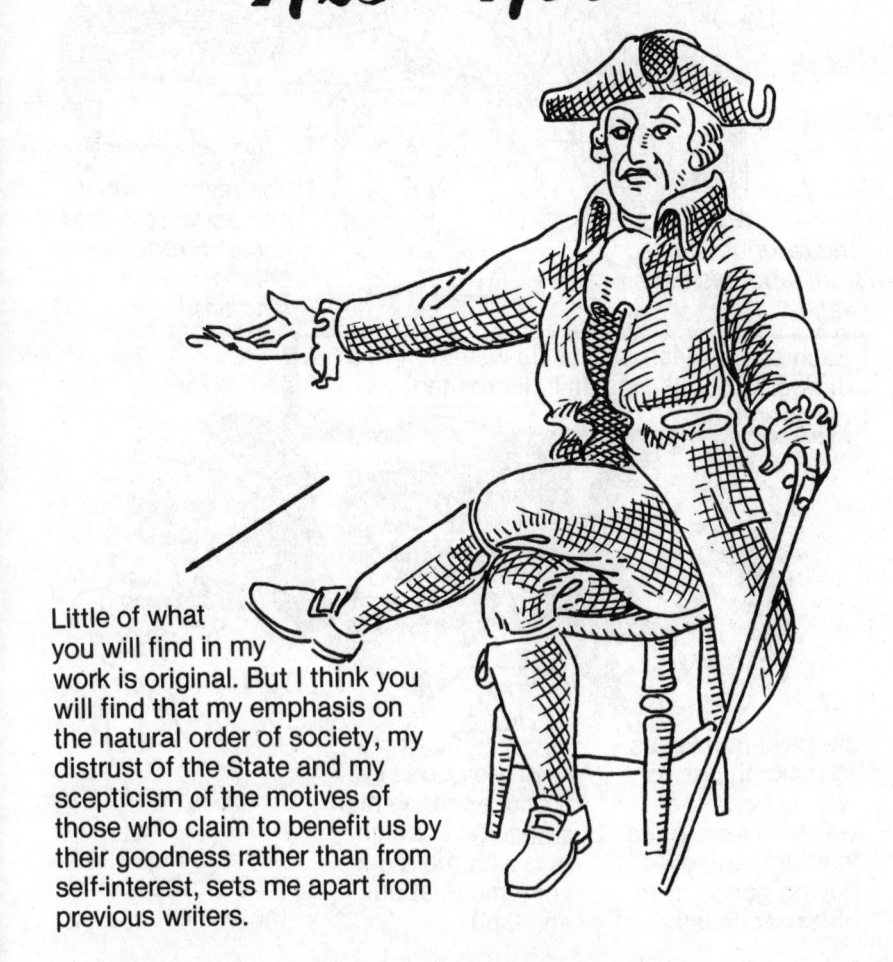

Little of what
you will find in my
work is original. But I think you
will find that my emphasis on
the natural order of society, my
distrust of the State and my
scepticism of the motives of
those who claim to benefit us by
their goodness rather than from
self-interest, sets me apart from
previous writers.

The Economic Classes

Adam Smith, in his **Wealth of Nations**, drew a distinction between the various economic classes in order to distinguish between those who produce wealth and those who consume it.

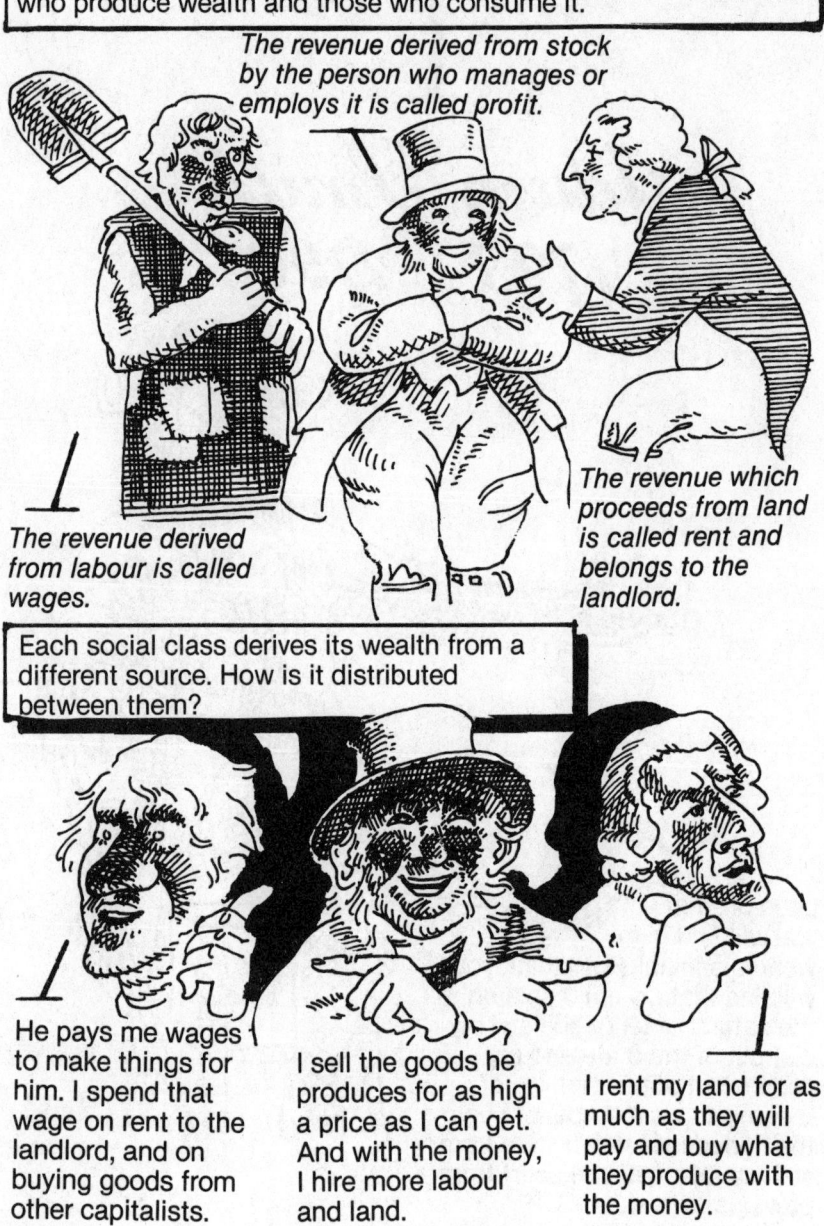

The revenue derived from stock by the person who manages or employs it is called profit.

The revenue derived from labour is called wages.

The revenue which proceeds from land is called rent and belongs to the landlord.

Each social class derives its wealth from a different source. How is it distributed between them?

He pays me wages to make things for him. I spend that wage on rent to the landlord, and on buying goods from other capitalists.

I sell the goods he produces for as high a price as I can get. And with the money, I hire more labour and land.

I rent my land for as much as they will pay and buy what they produce with the money.

Labour: Productive & Unproductive

Smith was concerned with identifying the social class that produced and increased the wealth of society. For it was clear that many who claimed to labour produced little for their efforts.

BLACKSMITH & IRON MANUFACTURER

HURRY UP, HIS MAJESTY'S WAITING.

The sovereign for example with all the officers both of justice and war who serve under him, the whole army and navy, are unproductive.

I, GEORGE III OF GREAT BRITAIN, IRELAND INC., HAVE ENOUGH TO DO, MR. SMITH, ENSURING A MARKET FOR OUR GOODS IN AMERICA WITHOUT PRODUCING THEM AS WELL.

The labour of the manufacturer fixes and realises itself in some particular subject or vendible commodity which lasts for some time, at least after the labour has passed.

It was this power of creating objects that maintain their value which distinguished productive from unproductive labour, and provides the basis for Smith's theory of value. But his emphasis on manufacture ignored all the services provided by the professions without which industry would grind to a halt.

The labour of the menial servant on the contrary does not fix or realise itself in any particular subject or vendible commodity. In the same class must be ranked some of the most frivolous professions, churchmen, lawyers, physicians, men of letters of all kinds; players, buffoons, musicians, opera-singers, etc.

I am the Lord High Justice,
This is the Vicar of Bray,
He's a Professor of Logic,
And we argue our time away.

We produce no exports,
We produce no stock,
We just legislate
and look after the State
'n see the boat **don't rock!**

For Smith, only capital in the form of investment in manufacture, and not land or services of any kind, is the real basis of wealth creation.

C'MON SMITH, PASS IT ON!

The Invisible Hand

The thrifty, industrious capitalist who spots an opportunity in the market for the employment of productive hands is the hero of Smith's work. In his efforts to increase his own wealth, he cannot do other but benefit society in general.

HERE'S A TOTALLY NEW INVENTION — A CAPITALIST SOCIAL BENEFIT MACHINE. YOU PUT INDIVIDUAL SELF-INTEREST IN THIS END AND SOCIAL BENEFITS COME OUT THE OTHER...

INDIVIDUAL INPUT

SOCIAL WELFARE

THIS TUBE'S FOR CAPITALIST PROFIT.

WONDERFUL! CAN WE TRY IT?

18

Amazing, isn't it?

In this state of things, the whole produce of labour does not always belong to the labourer. He must in most cases share it with the owner which employs it.

The Division of Labour

Having identified the social group that produced wealth, and the way this wealth tended to benefit the whole community, Smith then went on to describe the way it might be increased.

To take an example ...the trade of pinmaking...

one man draws out the wire, another straights it,

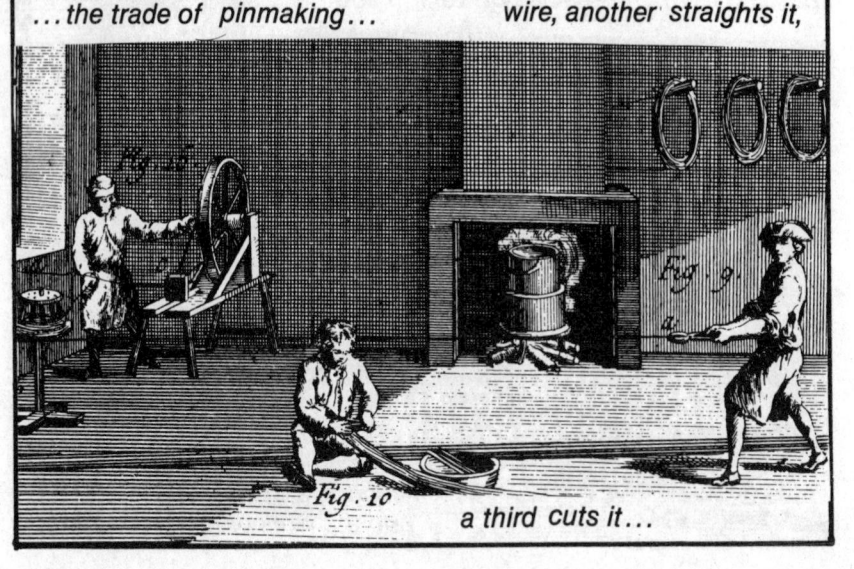

a third cuts it...

A fourth points it, a fifth grinds it at the top for receiving a head...and the important business of making a pin is, in this manner, divided into about eighteen distinct operations.

What is the benefit of having all these workers doing such a simple job?

First to increase the dexterity in every particular working man; secondly, to the saving of time which is commonly lost in passing from one species of work to another.

And lastly the invention of a great number of machines which facilitate and abridge labour, and enable one man to do the work of many.

In the cotton industry, for instance, this process of mechanisation, transformed the manufacture of cotton from a cottage into a factory industry.

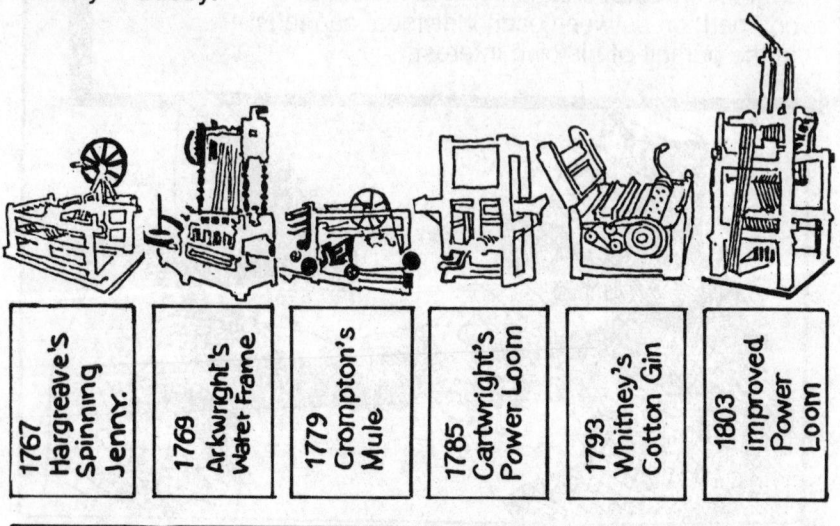

1767 Hargreave's Spinning Jenny.	1769 Arkwright's Water Frame	1779 Crompton's Mule	1785 Cartwright's Power Loom	1793 Whitney's Cotton Gin	1803 improved Power Loom

Smith placed little emphasis on this process of mechanisation, but contrasted the discipline of factory life with the easy going habits of handicraft cottage industry.

Every country workman who is obliged to change his work and tools every half hour is almost always slothful and lazy.

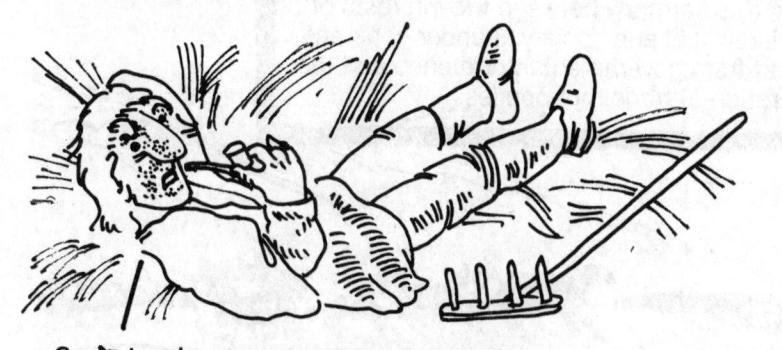

CAN'T decide WHETHER TO SHOE THE HORSE, MOW THE HAY, dig THE gArden, OR WHAT...
DECISIONS! DECISIONS!

The division of labour which depended on the size of the market was Smith's great engine of wealth creation. It was fuelled by competition between each individual capitalist in the pursuit of his own interest.

This division of labour, from which so many advantages are derived, is not originally the effect of any human wisdom, which foresees and intends that general opulence to which it gives occasion. It is the necessary, though very slow and gradual, consequence of a certain propensity... to truck, barter, and exchange one thing for another.

The social production of wealth that springs from this harmony between the interests of the individual and society is under constant threat from government interference and the operation of trade monopolies.

THAT SMITH DOESN'T LiKE GOVERNMENT...

Market Restraint: Monopoly

If a foreign country can supply us with a commodity cheaper than we can ourselves make it, better buy it off them with some part of the produce of our own industry employed in a way in which we have some advantage.

No regulation of commerce can increase the quantity of industry of any society beyond what its capital can maintain. It can only divert a part of it into a direction into which it might not otherwise have gone; and it is by no means certain that this artificial direction is likely to be more advantageous to the society than that which it would have gone on its own accord.

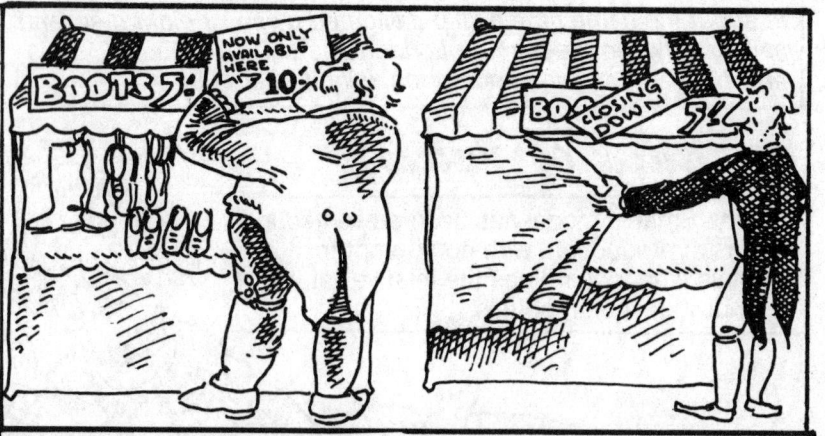

To give the monopoly of the home market to the produce of domestic industry in any particular art of manufacture, is in some measure to direct private people in the manner they ought to employ their capital, and must, in almost all cases, be either useless or hurtful regulation.

Market Restraint: Transport

But Smith did not stop with advocating the removal of restraints. He also looked towards the improvement of transport as a means of enlarging the market.

A broad wheeled wagon attended by two men and drawn by eight horses in about six weeks time carries and brings back between London and Edinburgh near four tons of goods.

In about the same time a ship navigated by six or eight men, and sailing between the ports of London and Leith frequently carries and brings back two hundred ton weight of goods.

Paradox of Value

So far, Smith's model has been presented in terms of production, with no attempt to explain what determines the relative values of individual commodities.

YOU STILL HAVEN'T EXPLAINED THE <u>PRICE</u> VALUE OF THINGS!

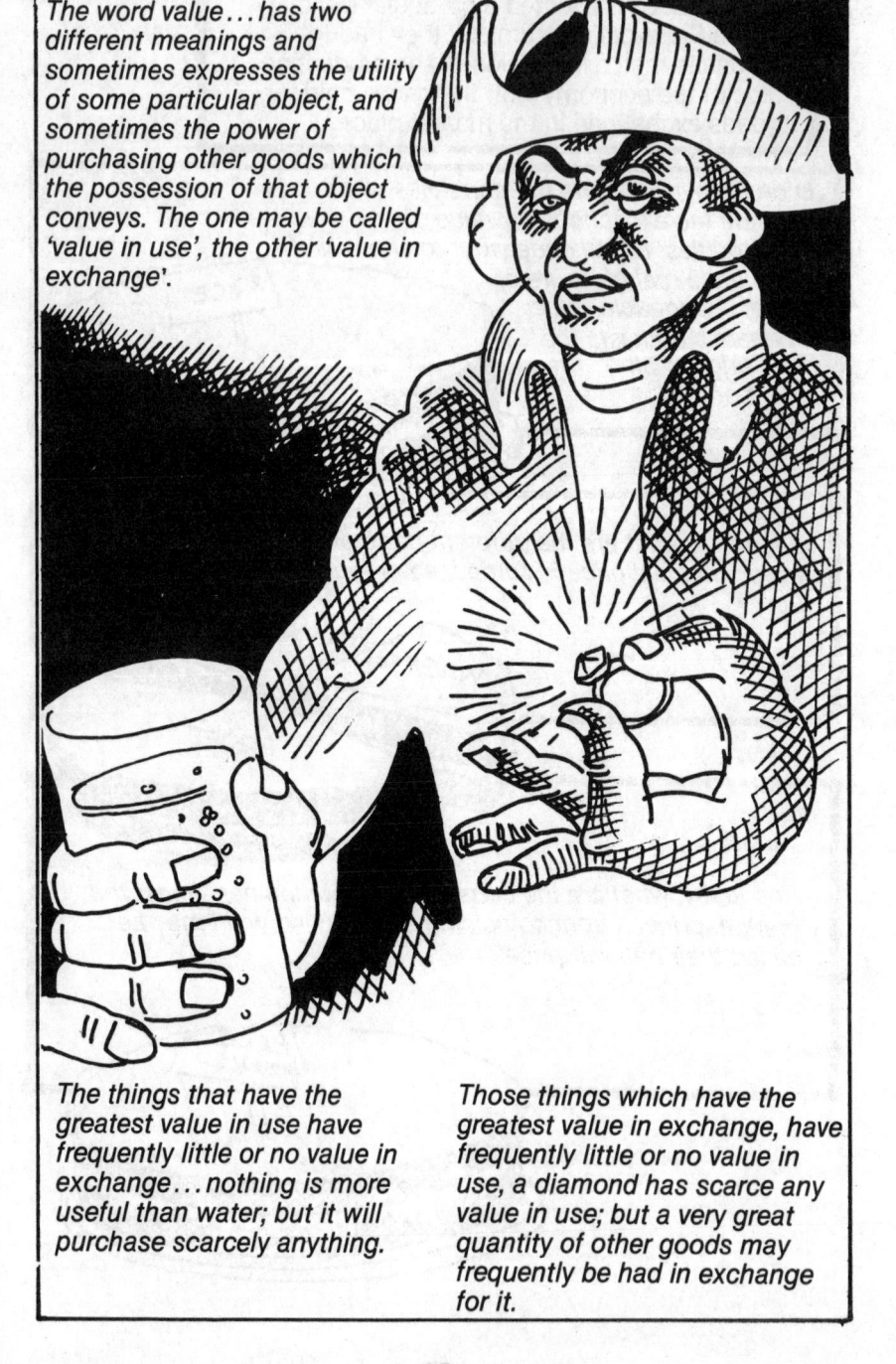

The word value...has two different meanings and sometimes expresses the utility of some particular object, and sometimes the power of purchasing other goods which the possession of that object conveys. The one may be called 'value in use', the other 'value in exchange'.

The things that have the greatest value in use have frequently little or no value in exchange...nothing is more useful than water; but it will purchase scarcely anything.

Those things which have the greatest value in exchange, have frequently little or no in use, a diamond has scarce any value in use; but a very great quantity of other goods may frequently be had in exchange for it.

This paradox presented a particular difficulty to the Classical economists: they had to reconcile their explanation of the production side of the economy with the prices paid for goods exchanged in the market place.

In order to investigate the principles which regulate the exchangeable value of commodities, I shall endeavour to show, first, what is the real measure of this exchangeable value; or wherein consists the real price of all commodities.

PRICE

Secondly, what are the different parts of which this real price is composed or made up.

WAGES · RENT · PROFIT

And lastly, what are the causes which sometimes hinder the market price... from coinciding exactly with what may be called their natural price?

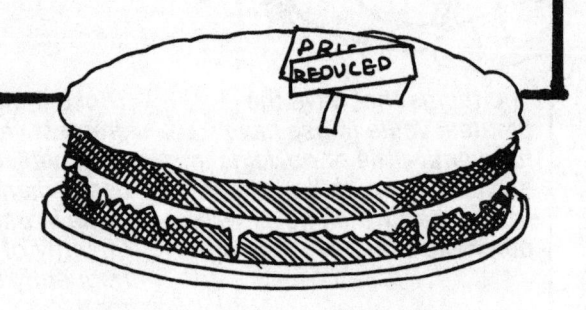

PRICE REDUCED

Labour Theory of Value I

Since wealth was created by productive labour, it was natural that Smith should develop a labour theory of value.

Labour… alone… never varying in its own value, is alone the ultimate and real standard by which the value of all commodities can at all times and places, be estimated and compared… equal quantities of labour, at all times and all places, may be said to be of equal value to the labourer.

So…? … WHY DO I HAVE TO SELL THE SHIRTS I MADE TODAY FOR HALF OF WHAT I SOLD THEM FOR LAST WEEK?

Smith tried to answer this awkward question by distinguishing between conditions in a primitive barter economy with no division of labour and an economy where the division of labour had taken place.

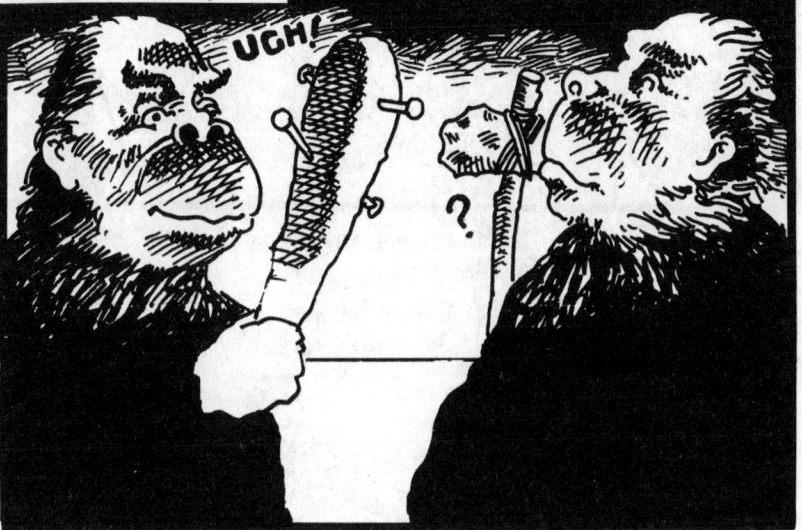

UGH!

?

If among a nation of hunters, for example, it usually costs twice the labour to kill a beaver which it does to kill a deer, one beaver should naturally exchange for, or be worth, two deer... in this state of things, the whole produce of labour belongs to the labourer.

But by the 18th century that accumulation of stock had already taken place through a variety of means which included loot from India, slave plantations, Dutch capital and family savings. And the equivalence of labour in exchange no longer existed.

Labour Theory of Value II

Smith in his modified theory of value admitted the claims of the capitalist and landlord with those of the labourer. The value of a commodity was no longer the amount of labour that went into its creation but the amount of labour it could command when exchanged – though from time to time Smith confused the two theories.

... he is rich or poor according to the quantity of labour which he may command.

I wish he'd make up his mind. There's a big difference between the amount of labour required to produce something, and what it might fetch on the market.

Natural Price/Market Price

In this **command** theory of value – which includes a return to the capitalist, the landlord, and the labourer – the natural price of a commodity is what is just sufficient to cover the average rates of profit, rent and wages prevailing in that area.

THE AVERAGE RENT IN THIS AREA FOR ENOUGH LAND TO GROW A BUSHEL OF WHEAT IS 20 SHILLINGS.

THE AVERAGE WAGE IN THIS AREA IS 20 SHILLINGS A WEEK.

AVERAGE PROFIT ON INDUSTRY IN THIS AREA IS ABOUT 20 SHILLINGS.

The actual price at which any commodity is commonly sold is called its market price. It may either be above, or below, or exactly the same with its natural price.

What am I offered for a bushel of wheat? –very short supply.

60 shillings.

70 shillings.

80 shillings.

Although Smith has shown how supply and demand may affect the natural price so that it no longer equals the sum of the capital, rent and wage it contains, he has yet to show how these factors themselves are determined.

Labour & Wages

Smith's account of the distribution of wealth between the economic classes is at times both sketchy and confused. In his explanation of what determines the amount of wages paid to labour he hints at several different causes but finally settles for a long-run subsistence theory.

If the wages of labour were ever more than sufficient to maintain the labourer and enable him to bring up a family, the competition of the labourers and the interest of the masters would soon reduce this to the lowest rate which is consistent with common humanity.

I decide what is consistent with humanity.

So wages are always mere subsistance.

Capital & Profit

My profit is affected by competition. Few capitalists: much profit!

The increase in stock which raises wages, tends to lower profits when the stock of many rich merchants are turned to the same trade. Their mutual competition naturally tends to lower profit; and when there is a like increase in stock in all the different trades carried on in the same society, the same competition must produce the same effect on all of them.

So as wealth increases in society, profit falls.

Get off! Look what you're doing to wages.

Land & Rent

Ana, I'm a landlord. We always get a bad press from Adam Smith.

As soon as the land of any country has all become private property, the landlords like all other men love to reap where they have never sown, and demand a rent even for its natural produce.

Rent, considered as the price for the use of land, is naturally the highest which the tenant can afford to pay in the circumstances of the land.

The rent of land is a monopoly price. It is not at all proportioned to what the landlord may have laid out upon the improvement of the land, or to what he can afford to take; but to what the farmer can afford to give.

Smith was suspicious of landlords and the role they played in the economy. But in the end he believed that there was a harmony between classes, for the landlord could only increase his rent if the wealth of the other classes was growing.

Smith develops a theory of rent that is differential and syphons off the extra income that a capitalist earns from higher than necessary pricing.

Why are your cabbages so expensive?

That's because I pay such high wages to produce them.

He always blames my wages for his high prices. In truth, M'lord it's because he adds so much profit to the price. But people still buy!

Oh, indeed? Well since he rents the land from me, he can afford a higher rent.

It is because high or low wages must be paid in order to bring a particular commodity to the market that its price must be high or low.

So you're making a lot of profit on the sale from the cabbage you grow on my land, so you can pay the higher rent I'm going to charge you!

But it is because its price is high or low; a great deal more, or very little more, or no more, than what is sufficient to pay those wages and profit, that it can afford a high rent, or a low rent, or no rent at all.

Behind Smith's economic harmony lay a profound suggestion of discord between the social classes. But it was left to Ricardo to explore this area.

There's more to Smith than meets the eye.

Summing up

Smith's message was that the free market brought about a harmony of economic interests between the classes, with the capitalist providing the motive force for the accumulation of wealth. Any interference with this harmony must inevitably result in reducing rather than increasing society's wealth.

Rent bears no relation to whether the landlord has invested anything in the improvement of the land or not; landlords, as monopolists, charge what they think the market will bear.

Capitalists rent land and hire labour to produce goods, and the profit they make from the sale of those goods is the residue left after they have paid wages and rent.

Only labour which produces tangible goods is productive. That which is engaged in services, or employed by landlords, does nothing to enlarge the wealth of society.

Productive labour produces more when specialised. And this specialisation, or division of labour, is dependent on the extent of the market.

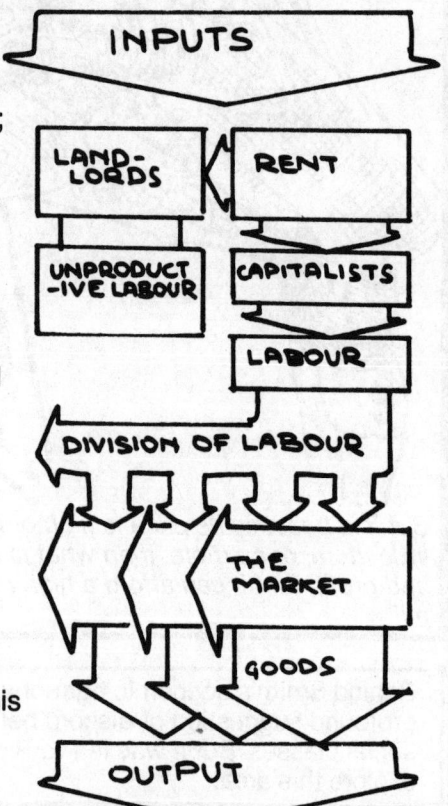

As the wealth of society increases, more people see the opportunity of hiring labour and land. More capitalists mean more competition and consequently profits fall. But the increase in society's wealth has the opposite effect on rent and wages. The competition between capitalists bids up wages, while the landlord as a monopolist demands more for his land.

2

David Ricardo
1772 1823

My efforts are not like Smith's to advocate Capitalism but to defend it. And my methods depend more on abstract analysis than on historical illustration.

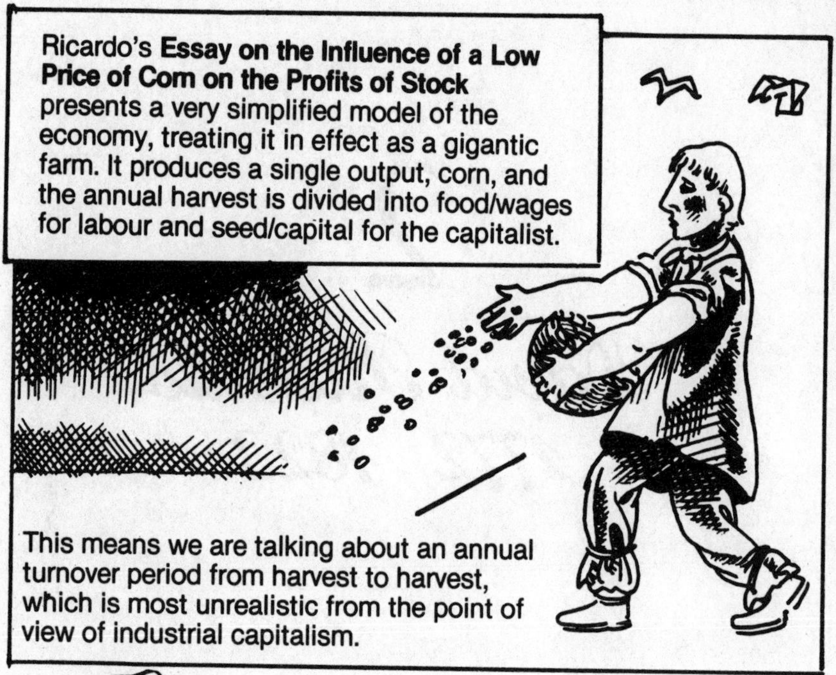

Ricardo's **Essay on the Influence of a Low Price of Corn on the Profits of Stock** presents a very simplified model of the economy, treating it in effect as a gigantic farm. It produces a single output, corn, and the annual harvest is divided into food/wages for labour and seed/capital for the capitalist.

This means we are talking about an annual turnover period from harvest to harvest, which is most unrealistic from the point of view of industrial capitalism.

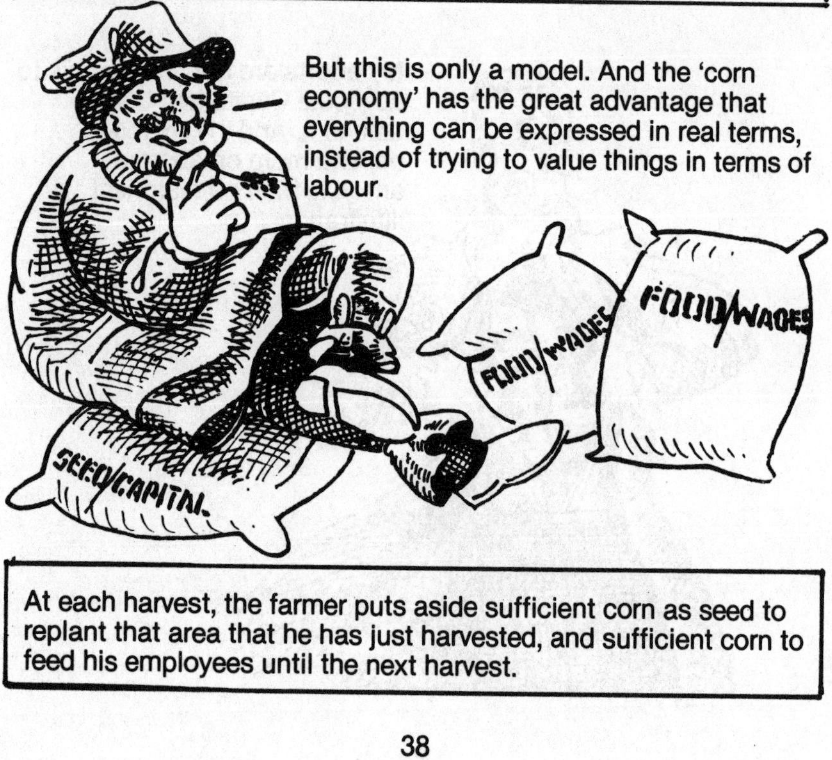

But this is only a model. And the 'corn economy' has the great advantage that everything can be expressed in real terms, instead of trying to value things in terms of labour.

FOOD/WAGES

FOOD/WAGES

SEED/CAPITAL

At each harvest, the farmer puts aside sufficient corn as seed to replant that area that he has just harvested, and sufficient corn to feed his employees until the next harvest.

38

Wage Fund

The number of men that the farmer can employ depends on the stock of corn he can invest. This is the origin of the notion of a Wage Fund – an idea later repudiated by Mill and Marx. In Ricardo's view, this wage fund should be sufficiently large to pay a conventional wage per man.

It is not to be understood that the natural price of labour, estimated even in food and necessities, is absolutely fixed and constant. It varies at different times in the same country, and very materially differs in different countries. It essentially depends on the habits and customs of the people.

But what about implements and investments on capital equipment? Where do I get these?

Well, we'll assume, for simplicity, that you make these during the winter from what you can find around the farm. As I say, this is only a model.

Differential Rent

The next claim on the harvest was the landlord. In England the landlords had long ago enclosed all common land and there were no fertile areas available without the payment of rent.

In the first settling of a country in which there is an abundance of rich and fertile land, there will be no rent.

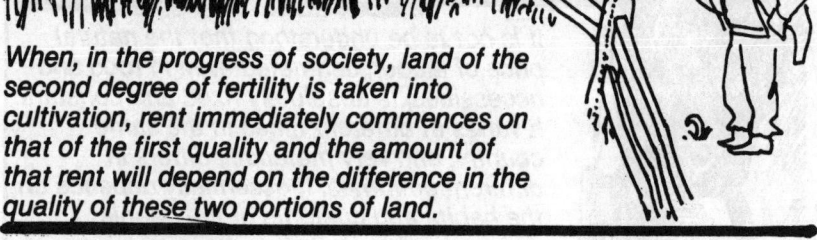

When, in the progress of society, land of the second degree of fertility is taken into cultivation, rent immediately commences on that of the first quality and the amount of that rent will depend on the difference in the quality of these two portions of land.

When land of the third quality is taken into cultivation, rent immediately commences on the second, and it is regulated as before by the differences in their productive powers.

Population expansion brings progressively poorer land under the plough, while competition for good land brings higher rents to landlords. But a ceiling on rent is provided by the fact that no farmer would pay more in rent than what he could gain in extra produce from the better land.

So far I've paid, out of this year's harvest, wages to labour and rent to the landlord, as well as put aside a stock of seed for next year's sowing which is termed capital. What I have left here is profit.

Corn Profit

The **rate of profit**, expressed as a percentage per annum, is profit per man divided by the wage necessary to employ a man, plus the seed he uses. This rate is the same for all farmers, since differences in output per man are offset by differential payments of rent.

How can any of us win this race if we are all handicapped to an extent which makes us all equal? It's unfair! After all, we are capitalists in competition.

Spring again; my stock of capital from last year's harvest determines how many men I employ.

The number of men I employ in turn determines the amount of land I cultivate.

The amount of land that is cultivated determines which quality of land at the margin is paying no rent.

GRADE 'A' LAND: HIGH RENT

All the factors accounted for and all done in **real** terms!

BAD OLD DAYS

PROFIT

Net output per head on the lowest quality of land in use, the wage being given by historic factors, determines profit per man employed.

GRADE 'A' HIGH RENT CORN

POOR LAND NO RENT CORN

And the level of rent is such as to make profit per man employed over the whole area equal to that on the no rent land.

POOR LAND NO RENT

GRADE 'B' LOW RENT LAND

Agricultural Profits Rule

In this model, profit in agriculture also determines profit levels in manufacture since all employers have to pay wages in corn. If manufacturers earned more profit than farmers, some farmers would abandon their farming for manufacturing; and if they earned less, some manufacturers would turn to farming.

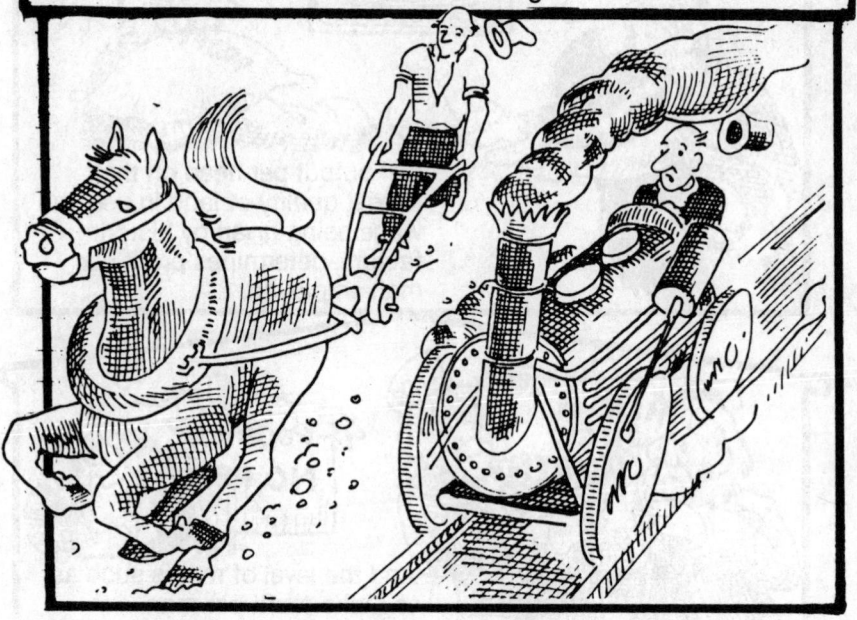

This means a single rate of profit operates throughout the economy.

Long Run Trend

Now we have the basic model, with an explanation as to how rent, wages and profits are determined. The problem is whether this system remains stable when operating over long periods. Ricardo was pessimistic about this for the following reasons.

CAPITAL

WAGES

The capitalist/farmer in an effort to expand his business may make some net investment by retaining a little extra corn from the previous harvest. This will enable him to employ more labour.

More labour means that poorer land will be taken into cultivation at the margin.

And as poorer land comes into cultivation, the differential rent on the good land rises through competition between the farmers.

Output per man, net of rent, diminishes. And since wages at subsistence cannot be cut, profits, as the residue after the payment of wages and rent, inevitably fall.

Falling Profit Rate

Profits depend on high or low wages...

Wages on the price of necessities...

And the price of necessities chiefly on the price of food.

The natural tendency of profits then is to fall; for, in the progress of society and wealth, the additional quantity of food required is obtained by the sacrifice of more and more labour.

Since the industrial sector is also linked to the agricultural through the assumption of a common 'corn wage', the rate of profit in both sectors falls.

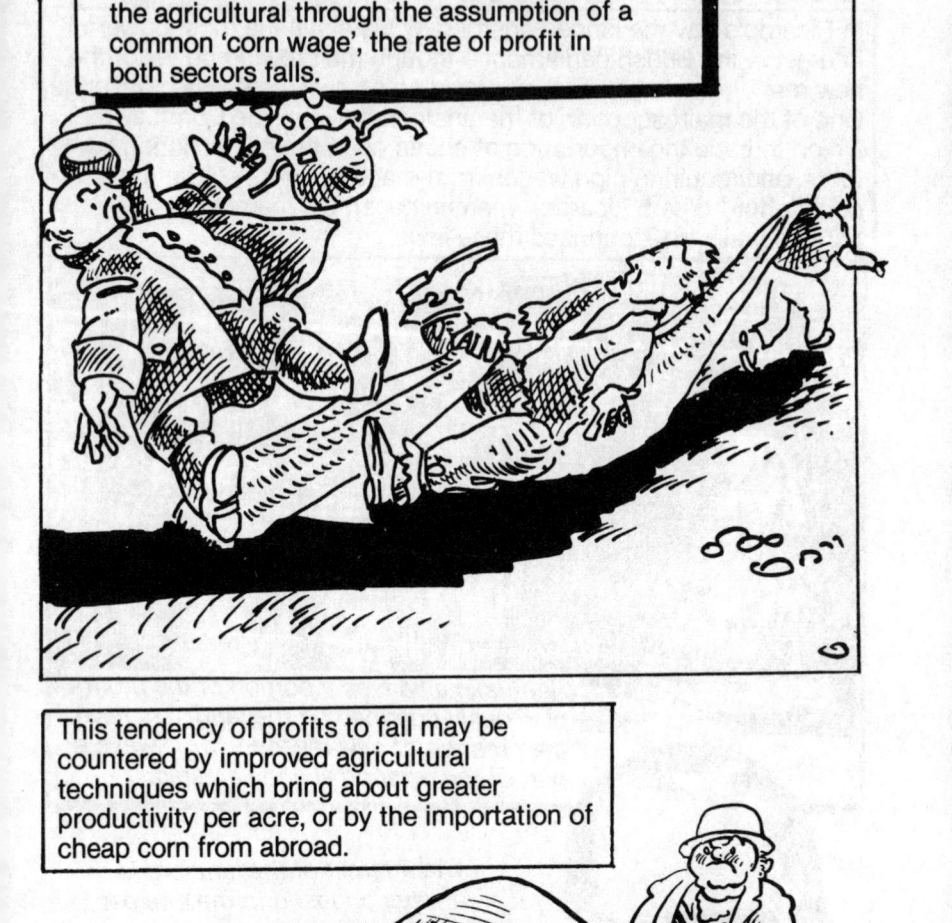

This tendency of profits to fall may be countered by improved agricultural techniques which bring about greater productivity per acre, or by the importation of cheap corn from abroad.

BEST U.S. CORN

The Corn Laws

In Ricardo's day the landed aristocracy were still the most powerful interest in the British parliament – though the growing power of the new manufacturing class was providing an ever-increasing challenge. One of the main supports of the aristocracy were the Corn Laws which forbade the importation of cheap corn, thereby ensuring high rents, and requiring high wages from manufacturers so that labour could afford bread. Ricardo, when he became a member of parliament in 1819, opposed these laws.

Rent is in all cases a portion of the profits previously obtained on the land. It is never the creation of new revenue, but always a part of the revenue already created.

The interest of the landlord is always opposed to the interest of every other class in the community. His situation is never more prosperous as when food is scarce and dear; whereas, all other persons are greatly benefited by procuring cheap food.

The Corn Laws were eventually repealed in 1846.

Thomas Malthus, Ricardo's friend and one of the staunchest defenders of the landlord's interest, made several damaging comments on some of the assumptions behind the model.

So what's your point, Malthus?

You're model is unreal, Ricardo.

Malthusian Objection I

Profit cannot be calculated in corn terms in the real world. There is no section of the economy with single commodity (corn) inputs. Wages consist of some manufactured and imported goods, so any calculation of profit will involve combining different groups of goods which comprise output, wages and investment.

Corn on the cob, corn flakes, corn flour, I'm sick of corn! I want something else!

If you don't accept this corn as payment, you're going to make life very difficult for Ricardo.

My dear Malthus, in an effort to make my corn model more realistic, I want to first draw a distinction between scarce and produced commodities. While the value of scarce commodities is determined by the demand made on a fixed supply, the price of produced commodities depends on the inducement to capitalists to manufacture them – namely, the rate of profit.

Commodities: Produced / Scarce

There are some commodities, the value of which is determined by their scarcity alone. No labour can increase the quantity of such goods, and therefore their value cannot be lowered by increased supply.

You may recall my problem with the paradox of value.

These commodities, however, form a very small part of the mass of commodities daily exchanged on the market. By far the greater part of those goods which are the object of desire are procured by labour; and may be multiplied...almost without assignable limit.

In speaking, then, of commodities, of exchangeable value, and of the laws which regulate their relative prices, we mean always such commodities only as can be increased in quantity by the exertion of human industry.

Interdependence of Prices & Profit

The price that these commodities are sold for must cover both the subsistence wage of the labourer and profit to the capitalist which is uniform for all lines of production.

So both wages and profit are determined across the whole economy?

Yes, and the reason for the differences in prices between commodities is the fact that different products require different amounts of capital to produce and take different lengths of time before they show a return.

First of all we find the **profit rate** which is the amount of profit earned per annum divided by the value of the investment required for production.

If our profit rates differed, we'd move into each others' trades.

If, as Ricardo maintains, the general rate of profit falls with a fall in agricultural profit rate on marginal land...

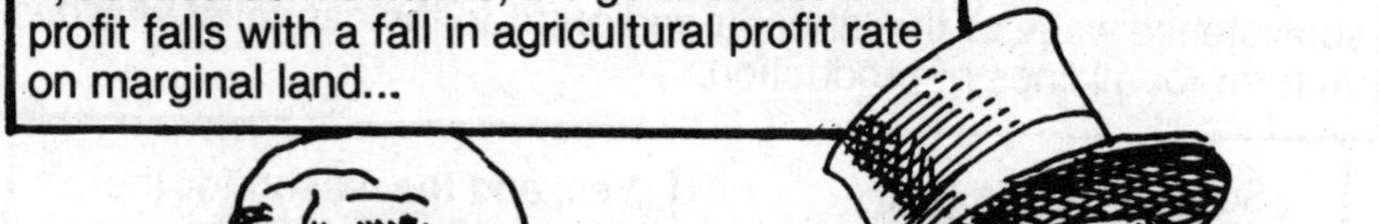

The profit rate has fallen and I have to divide this between my four men and materials, so I have to raise my prices.

The fall in profit rate hasn't affected me to the same extent since I have only one man employed in my manufacturing. I don't have to raise my price as much as he.

It is clear that a fall in the general fall of profit rate will alter relative prices by raising the price of labour-intensive to capital-intensive products.

But I thought that only higher productivity from labour would alter the price of any commodity relative to its neighbour.

So far we've been working under the assumption that wages to labour remain at subsistence, but if we relax this assumption, then it will be impossible to know whether it is a wage rise or profit rise that is responsible for a change of relative prices and the proportion of the change.

That is why I want to find an invariable measure of value.

An Invariable Measure

In an effort to overcome this interdependence between profit and prices, Ricardo now sought an **invariable standard** which would replace corn in his simple model. He tried a labour theory of value but abandoned it. Later he tried to make gold fulfil this role, but again without success.

The only qualities necessary to make a measure of value a perfect one are, that it should itself have value, and that that value should be itself invariable.

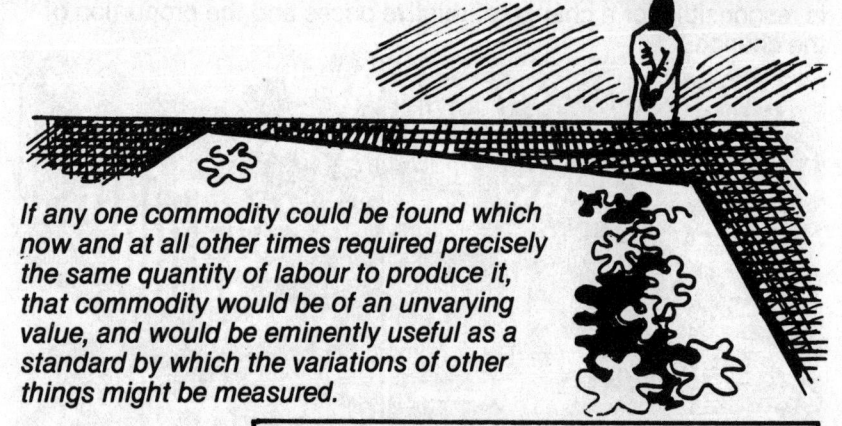

If any one commodity could be found which now and at all other times required precisely the same quantity of labour to produce it, that commodity would be of an unvarying value, and would be eminently useful as a standard by which the variations of other things might be measured.

He was still trying to find such a measure at his death.

Malthusian Objection II

The second substantial objection made by Malthus against Ricardo's system was that the accumulation of the capitalists, and the resulting increase in their productive powers under the influence of competition, would result in more being produced than could be sold.

Is there demand for all that the capitalists produce?

Produce! Produce! Produce! That's what the capitalist system is all about. But who's going to consume all this? Where are people to get the money to buy all this stuff?

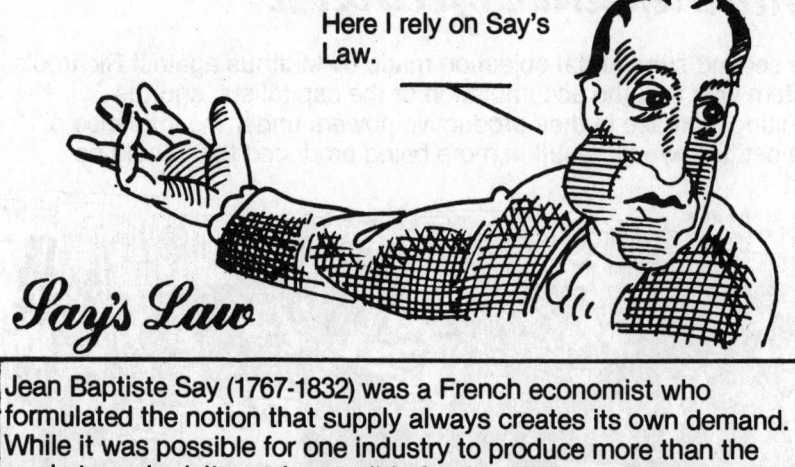

Here I rely on Say's Law.

Say's Law

Jean Baptiste Say (1767-1832) was a French economist who formulated the notion that supply always creates its own demand. While it was possible for one industry to produce more than the market required, it was impossible for the whole economy to overproduce, because aggregate demand and aggregate supply are not independent of one another.

There is no amount of capital which may not be employed in a country, because demand is only limited by production.

No man produces, but with a view to consume or sell, and he never sells, but with an intention to purchase some other commodity.

By producing, then, he necessarily becomes either the consumer of his own goods, or the purchaser and consumer of the goods of some other person.

Too much of a particular commodity may be produced of which there may be a glut in the market so as not repay the capital expended on it; but this cannot be the case with respect to all commodities.

This doctrine dominated the mainstream of economic theory until the publication of Keynes' General Theory. Only Malthus challenged it, and his analysis was insufficient to overthrow this view.

57

Summing up

Say's Law provided the main defence for Ricardo and the Classical economists against the view that the capitalist system tended towards over-production. Those who held this view, Malthus, Marx and others, made little headway against the orthodoxy of the Ricardian tradition. It was not until the massive slump of the 1930s – nearly a century later – that economists were forced to look seriously at this question again.

The turnover period in Ricardo's **corn model** was annual, based on the harvest cycle.

The quality and yield of the poorest land determined the rent on all other land.

Rent was a monopoly price that had to be paid before production could commence.

The residue of produce that is left to the capitalist after he has paid rent, wages and **invested** for the following year's capital/seed, is his profit.

Labour is paid a subsistence wage determined by historical factors.

The level of profit in the industrial sector controls the profit level in the agricultural so that they are both equal.

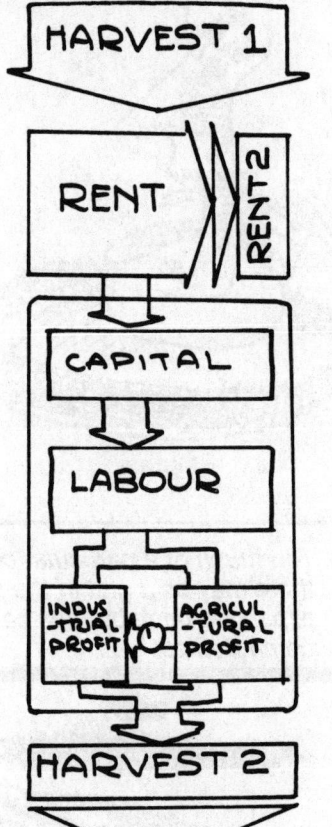

Ricardo's conclusions followed from a few abstract principles, and the political lessons drawn from them were used by radicals to attack the landowning class as an unnecessary economic burden on society's wealth. Any defence of this class in the future would have to use the same rigorous analysis that Ricardo employed, and the first and foremost defender appeared in Ricardo's own lifetime.

3

Thomas Malthus
1766 1834

Ricardo is wrong. He doesn't realise that his capitalist system has fatal flaws – it depends on that aristocracy he's so busy attacking! My enquiry is more into the poverty of nations rather than their wealth. It is an explicit attack on the Radicalism that follows from Ricardo's economic theory.

Malthus' father sympathised with the ideas of the perfectability of man that influenced the leaders of the French Revolution. Malthus reacted against this and was an avowed opponent of attempts to improve the lot of the mass of humanity. His first step was to construct an argument to show how impossible and misconceived such a project was...

Impossible!

I think I may fairly make two postulata. First, that food is necessary to the existence of man.

Secondly, that the passion between the sexes is necessary and will remain nearly at its present state.

The Population Principle

Assuming that my postulata be granted, I say that the power of population is infinitely greater than the power of the earth to produce food.

Population, when unchecked, increases in a geometrical ratio...

Subsistence increases only in an arithmetical ratio...

A slight acquaintance with numbers will show the immensity of the first power in comparison with the second.

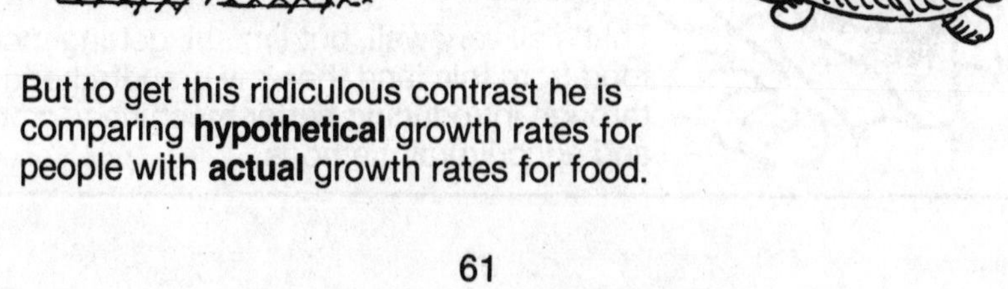

But to get this ridiculous contrast he is comparing **hypothetical** growth rates for people with **actual** growth rates for food.

Diminishing Returns

Since population always tends to outstrip food supply, why aren't more people dying of starvation?

Any why isn't the world one solid mass of flesh?

I said population would grow only if _unchecked!_

Malthus then went on to give his reasons as to why population did not grow at the rate his theory might have suggested. Various forms of checks operated which he classified as preventative and positive. Under the category of preventative checks, Malthus included all forms of contraceptives and methods of artificially limiting the birth rate which he condemned as improper.

It's improper. It's worse —its vice

The alternative to birth control methods were the harsh effects of positive checks.

The positive checks on population include all the causes which tend in any way to shorten the duration of human life, such as unwholesome occupations, severe labour and exposure to the seasons, bad nursing for children, excesses of all kinds, great towns and manufacturies, the whole train of common diseases and epidemics, wars, infanticide, plague and famine... those positive checks which appear to arise from the law of nature may be called exclusively misery.

Do you promise to keep this woman in the poverty she is accustomed to?

You bet! We'll fix that by having plenty of children!

Social Restraint

The only acceptable alternative was late marriage and self-restraint.

Gad, this economics is a very Puritan business!

Malthusian Social Policy

But however great the misery of the poor, Malthus opposed any scheme for the redistribution of wealth or for the alleviation of poverty. He was a vigorous opponent of the Poor Laws which gave limited help to the poor of each parish.

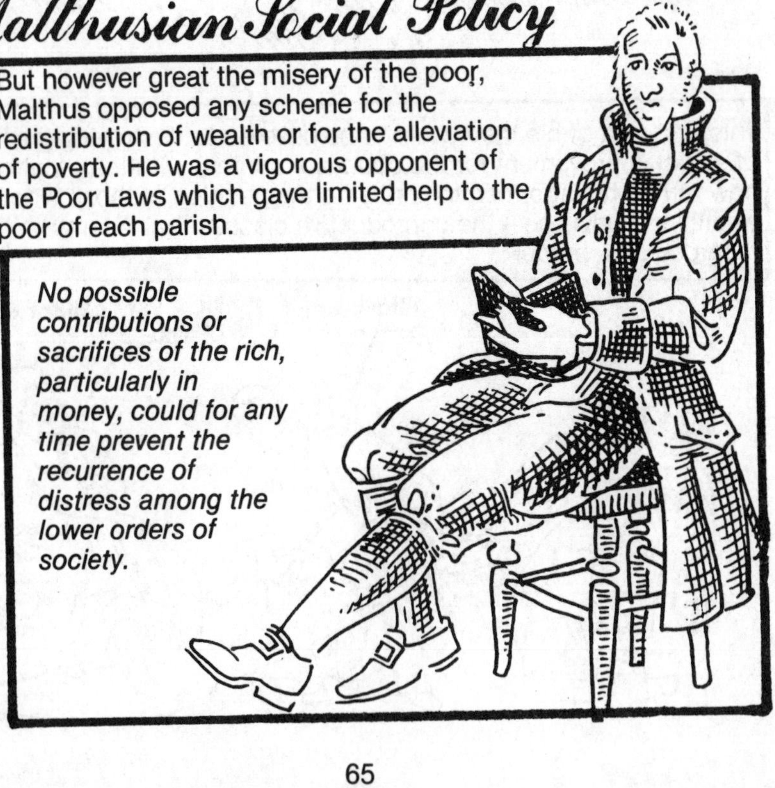

No possible contributions or sacrifices of the rich, particularly in money, could for any time prevent the recurrence of distress among the lower orders of society.

> The rich might become poor and some of the poor rich, but a part of society must necessarily feel difficulty in living, and this difficulty will naturally fall on the least fortunate members of society.

This first part of his theory had to be devoted to destroying the basis of social improvement for the poor. Not content with that, Malthus now turned his attention to justifying the position of those who had wealth and privilege – the unproductive classes that Adam Smith had regarded as a burden.

Effective Demand

The next part of his strategy was to take over Smith's cost of production theory, which you'll remember defined value as the amount of stored and current labour in a commodity – plus profit. Profit had been added by the capitalist to value, with the result that labour could not afford to pay for the goods it created.

Get on with it lad.
You've only made
one pair of boots
this week

So? You've only paid
me one shilling!

Here's my shilling
for a pair of boots.

Sorry, lad, boots
are one shilling and
sixpence a pair.

TRADESMENS
ENTRANCE

HIGH CLASS SHOES

BOOTMAKER

The productive elements in society could not alone provide effective demand for what they produce.

But this is an argument for redistributing wealth!

Not if you take the view that the equalisation of wealth, and the consequent rise in effective demand, would mean that humanity would multiply itself up to the point of starvation.

Malthus then looked at how effective demand was distributed between the economic classes, since without effective demand there could be no economic growth. And economic growth was at the back of all Classical economic theories.

Labour has insufficient spending power to ensure an expanding economy with more industry and wealth. Paying them higher wages would only mean that they would increase their numbers.

While the disposition of the capitalists was to save rather than spend, so they were no guarantee against stagnation either!

Unproductive Labour

It is absolutely necessary that a country with great powers of production should possess a body of unproductive consumers.

WANTED FOR IMMEDIATE EMPLOYMENT: UNPRODUCTIVE CLASS WHO THINK BIG OWNING AT LEAST 94% OF THE COUNTRY'S WEALTH NO LABOURERS NEED APPLY

Will we do? We're landlords.

We have twelve thousand acres,
Eleven dozen servants,
Ten great estates,
Nine lesser mansions,
Eight town houses,
Seven praying parsons,
Six daughters' dowries,
Five wastrel sons,
Four rotten boroughs,
Three grand tours,
Too much taxation

And a regiment of soldiers...

Just what the economy needs!

With that analysis of the spending power of the three classes, Malthus was able to show that gluts of unsold goods could arise from 'under-consumption' – a fact thought impossible by Classical economists who accepted Say's Law.

Gluts

If the creation of wealth depends on the unproductive classes, mainly landlords...then it follows that wherever that class is too poor, or where the productive powers of society have increased beyond their requirements, a surplus of goods will build up that cannot be sold.

And the result is bankruptcy for the capitalist and unemployment for the labourer.

Overproduction is not something that affects a single industry, as the followers of Say maintained. It affects the **whole** economy. Since the demand of this relatively small, but crucial, class is easily saturated, the economy plunges from boom to slump under its influence.

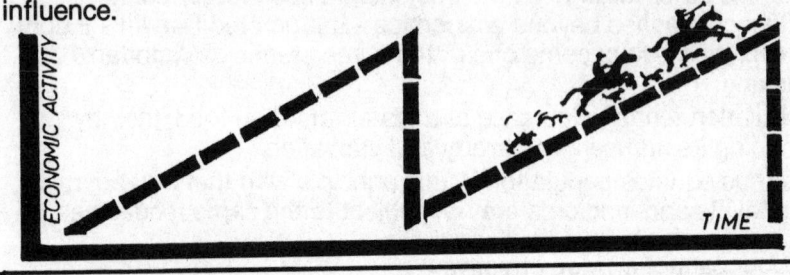

Malthus debated his notion of underconsumption with his friend Ricardo, whose system, as we have seen, did not depend on the existence of an unproductive élite.

Capitalists invest in machinery which produces even more goods. But if labourers have to forego consumption ·where is the demand for these extra goods to come from?

My dear Malthus, machines are made by labour too. Capitalist investment has merely transferred effective demand from one set of labourers to another. The power to consume has not been annihilated.

Summing up

Malthus' Principle of Population dominated economic theory long after his other writings on the subject had been forgotten. Its influence reached beyond economics – it prompted Darwin's theory of evolution – to become one of the cornerstones of Victorian thinking.

Population tends to increase at a faster rate than food, thereby reducing its numbers to poverty and starvation.

Malthus equates population in this principle with that of labour; capitalists and landlords are not subject to the same tendencies.

Labour cannot provide effective demand for manufactured goods since the perpetual increase in its numbers eliminates any surplus it might have.

Since capitalists are reluctant to spend, the only class that can provide effective demand are landlords.

The Malthusian theory of distribution can be more accurately described as one of non-distribution. Labour produces too many children; capitalists produce too many goods; and landlords are a necessary but not sufficient means of ensuring that the economic mechanism does at least function, even if only fitfully.

Malthusian theory provided a variety of arguments. It gave economic justification to a social class that was totally unproductive. It showed that capitalism as envisaged by Smith and Ricardo is not a self-adjusting system. Yet it also argued that any attempt to interfere with the market mechanism in order to overcome this instability is doomed to failure, since the population principle defeated all attempts to control it. It was against these assumptions that the next two writers – Mill and Marx – directed their efforts.

4

John Stuart Mill
1806 1873

I have tried to tame the capitalist system outlined in classical economics.

John Stuart Mill wrote one of the most influential textbooks on economics of the 19th century. It was used by students in Britain and America from its publication in 1848 till the end of the century. Mill attempted to marry a variety of ideas from Smith, Ricardo, Say and Malthus with radical sentiments for the more equitable distribution of wealth. Many felt this project to be impossible, and saw in Mill a radical struggling against a conservative and outdated economic tradition.

Rent

Rent is the difference between the unequal returns of different parts of capital employed on the land.

Profit

I define profit as depending exclusively on wages, being the difference between the wages paid to labour and the value of labour's product.

That is the most perfect form in which the theory of profits seems to have been exhibited.

Population

Mill held rigidly to the Malthusian view that population increases at the expense of wealth.

The Wage Fund

This led him to endorse the view common among his contemporaries that there was a strict limit set to the total funds available for wages.

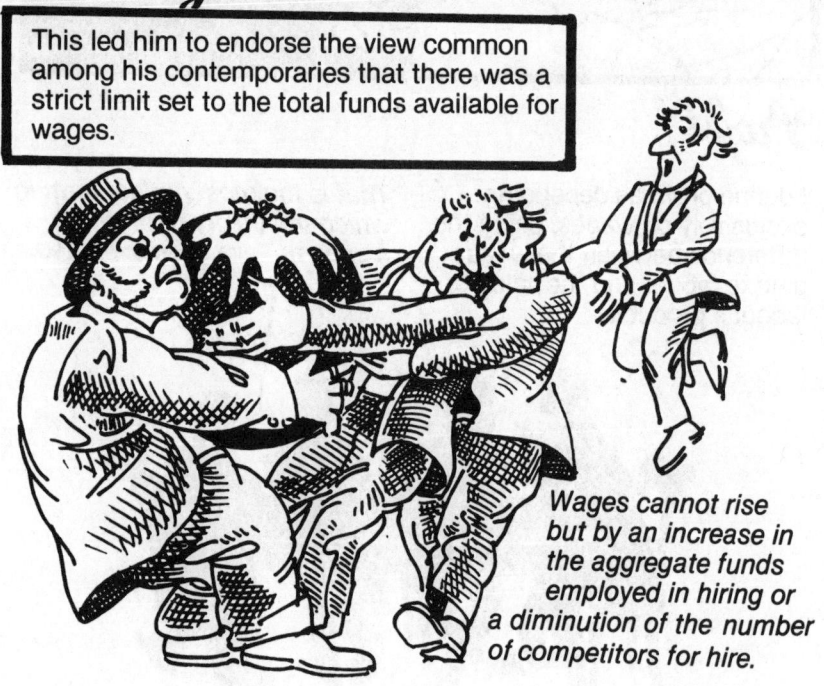

Wages cannot rise but by an increase in the aggregate funds employed in hiring or a diminution of the number of competitors for hire.

Mill recanted this doctrine later in life when it was shown that no such entity existed. The real limit on wages was not such a fund, but the practical consideration by the capitalist as to how much he can afford to pay in wages.

I was wrong.

Value

Mill accepted Smith's theory of value as a summing-up of rent, wages and profit.

MARGINALISM

Happily, there is nothing in the laws of value which remains to be cleared up; the theory of the subject is complete.

In the light of subsequent developments, this statement appears rather premature.

Productive Labour & Services

But on a variety of other points, Mill broke with the Classical tradition. He rejected Smith's distinction between productive and unproductive labour.

Labour is not creative of objects, but of utilities. Why should not all labour which produces utility be accounted productive?

You'll hear more about utility from me, Alfred Marshall.

> Why refuse the title to the surgeon who sets a limb, the judge and legislator who confer security, and give it to a lapidary who cuts and polishes a diamond?

Production & Distribution

Mill also tried to disengage the capitalist production system from the debate about distribution.

> The laws and conditions of the production of wealth partake of the character of physical truths. Whatever mankind produces, must be produced in the modes and under the conditions imposed by the constitution of external things.

It is not so with the distribution of wealth, that is a matter of human distribution solely. The distribution of wealth depends on the laws and customs of society; the rules by which it is determined are what the opinions and feeling of the ruling portion make them.

Does this mean government can interfere with the smooth operation of the market mechanism?

Does this mean social legislation will insure we aren't exploited for his benefit?

Interest & Abstinence

If this was the first attempt by a leading economist to grant that wealth might be distributed on different principles, there were many others in society who challenged the prevailing system.

Mill's dilemma was that in questioning capitalist distribution, how could capitalist profit or interest be justified at all?

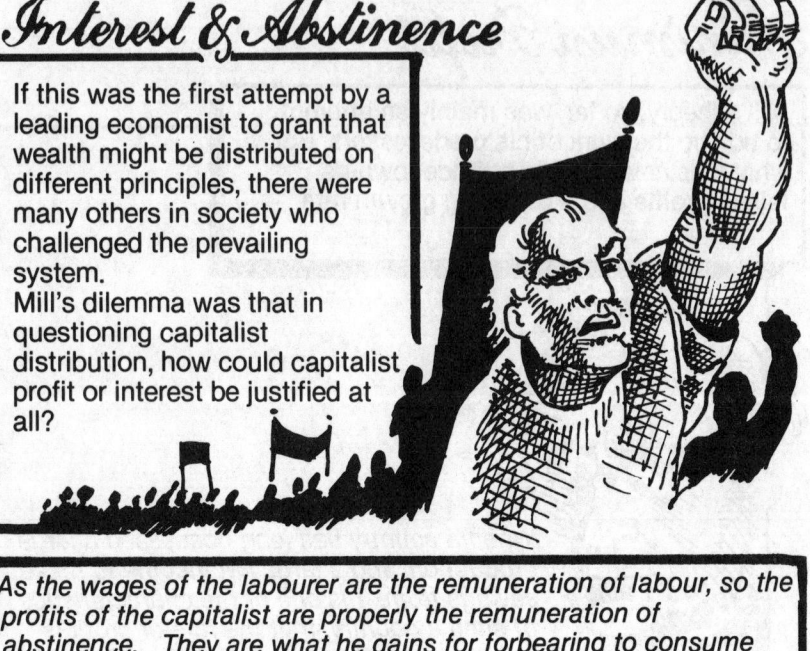

As the wages of the labourer are the remuneration of labour, so the profits of the capitalist are properly the remuneration of abstinence. They are what he gains for forbearing to consume his capital for his use, and allowing it to be consumed by productive labourers for their uses.

If I don't eat this plate of corn, but lend it to you instead, I'll want it back later with interest.

I wonder what he means by 'lend' and 'interest'? Gulp!

Minimun Profit

Mill's theory, so far, was mainly an attempt to tidy up the work of his predecessors. But what was new was his attitude towards falling profits and a declining growth rate.

When a country has long possessed a large production, and a large net income to make savings from, it is one of the characteristics of such a country, that the rate of profit is habitually within as it were a hair's breadth of the minimum, and that country is on the very verge of the stationary state.

SORRY, NOT TEMPTING ENOUGH!

PROFIT

There is at every time and place some particular rate of profit, which is the lowest that will induce the people of that country and time to accumulate savings and to employ those savings productively.

The Stationary State

Although this tendency towards a stationary state was inevitable as the rate of profit declined in mature economies, Mill regarded the trend with a certain amount of cautious optimism. He held the view, now identified with Galbraith among others, that it was the underdeveloped countries that needed growth more than the industrialised.

It is only in the backward countries of the world that increased production is still an important object. In those most advanced what is economically needed is better distribution.

Social Criticism

Mill was against the social competition between individuals for wealth, and saw in American society a particularly harsh example of this struggle.

I confess I am not charged with the ideal of life held out by those who think that the normal state of human beings is that of struggling to get on; that the trampling, crushing, elbowing and treading on each others heels, which forms the existing type of social life, are the most desirable lot of mankind.

Mill then went on to outline the kind of Socialism which might take the place of the existing system.

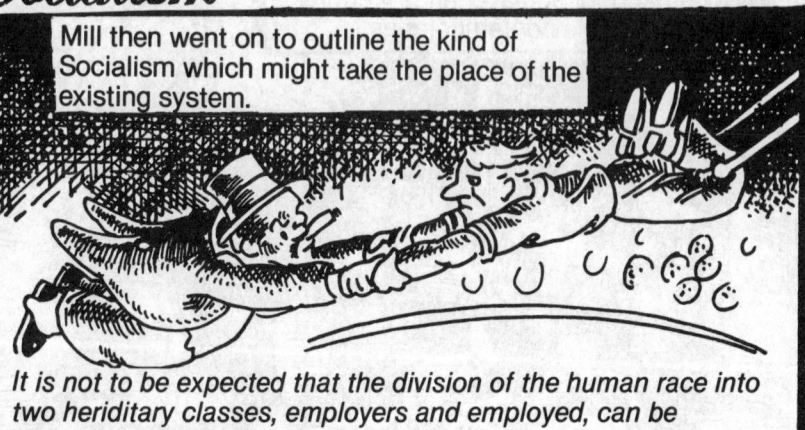

It is not to be expected that the division of the human race into two heriditary classes, employers and employed, can be permanently maintained.

There can be little doubt that the relations of masters and work people will be gradually superceeded by partnerships in one or two forms; in some cases, association of the labourers with the capitalists; in others, and perhaps finally in all, association of labourers among themselves.

But Mill gave little guidance as to how this partnership might come about. He was still wedded to the economic doctrines of competition and Smith's 'invisible hand' of self-interest, and on these foundations it was impossible to build any form of socialism.

Mill's demand for social change went far beyond that of his contemporaries.

...THE RED FLAG FLYING HERE...

If the institution of private property necessarily carried with it as a consequence, that the produce of labour should be apportioned as we now see it, almost in an inverse ratio to labour... if this or communism were the alternative, all the difficulties, great or small, of communism would be as dust in the balance.

Reservations

But he always sought to reconcile individual liberty with collectivist principles.

Laissez faire... should be the general practice; every departure from it, unless required by some great good, is a certain evil.

Although Mill regarded himself as carrying on the work of Adam Smith and Ricardo, the social framework had changed much in the intervening years. The arguments in **The Wealth of Nations** were against mercantilism and monopolies. But the political struggle in Mill's day was between collectivism and competition and, although he recognised that there were many areas for which the market system was unable to provide, he was reluctant to concede a role to the State.

Education was a prime example in this field. Mill accepted that government would have to provide some funds, but he would not have accepted the principle of free public education.

Summing up

Mill regarded himself as a disciple of Ricardo. Although he started from Ricardian premises, he took that system far beyond what its founder would have recognised and introduced so many original ideas on the way that he fashioned it into a system of his own.

He placed a new emphasis on utility, or the subjective element, rather than the harsher forces of necessity so frequently found in the Classical system. His use of this concept was particularly important in his definition of productive labour to include service industry as well as manufacturing.

It also led him to emphasise the balance between the forces of supply and demand, and at several points in his system he brings this mechanism into play.

His theory of interest was also original, but his main claims as an economist lie outside the sphere of distribution and value in the sphere of international trade.

His separation of production from distribution gave him the opportunity to introduce a plea for a more equitable distribution of the wealth produced between labour and capital.

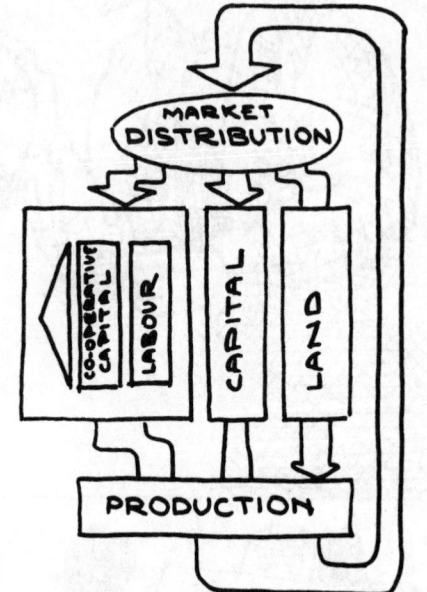

Mill was less successful in his attempt to reconcile this programme of reform with his belief in laissez-faire economic policy. His main suggestion was for a partnership between capital and labour in the form of co-operatives, but he provided very little analysis as to how this would operate in reality. It was left to his contemporary, Karl Marx, to provide a more thorough-going economic reappraisal of the relation between capital and labour.

5

Karl Marx
1818   1883

Workmen of the
world, unite. You
have nothing to lose
but your chains.

CAPITAL
VOL. I

Karl Marx began his investigations into Political Economy as a continuation of his philosophical and social critique of capitalism. His economics was only a part, but a very important part, of an all-embracing theory of historical change. This interest in the dynamics of economic change was something new, and most of **Capital**, the massive work which he began in 1859 and was still working on at the time of his death in 1883, was devoted to showing the origin, growth and future trends of capitalism.

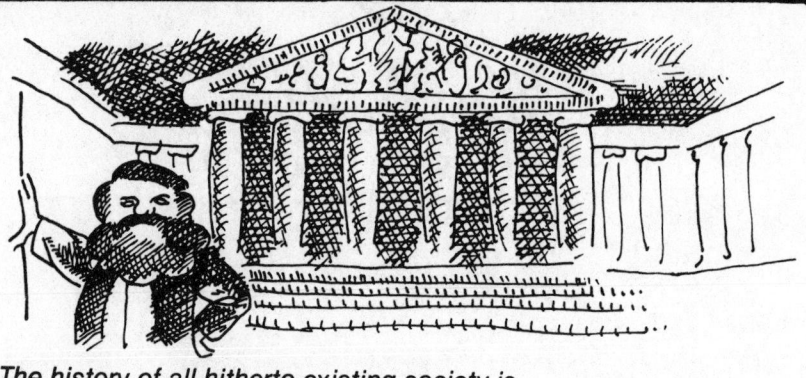

The history of all hitherto existing society is the history of class struggle.

In ancient Rome we have patricians, knights, plebeians, slaves...

In the middle ages feudal lords, vassals, guildmasters, journeymen, apprentices, serfs; in almost all those classes again, subordinate gradations...

The modern bourgeois society that has sprouted from the ruins of feudal society has not done away with class antagonism. It has established new classes, new conditions of oppression, new forms of struggle.

Commodities

This perpetual class war is between those classes who work to produce goods and those who own the land or machines used in this production. The owners of the means of production extract from the slave, or the serf, by the direct threat of force. But capitalism was based on a free contract between the employee and the employer, so how under these conditions could there be exploitation or class struggle?

If I paid him less than the market value, he'd take up work with my competitor who'd pay him more. Or he could go into business for himself.

The problem Marx set himself was to tear away the veil from capitalist exploitation. The first step towards understanding this process was to look at the basic unit of capitalist exchange, the **commodity**, to which everything was sooner or later reduced.

A commodity is in the first place an object outside of us, a thing that by its properties satisfies human want of some sort or other.

USEFUL BRUSH MAKERS & SON

WORK MEN'S ENTRANCE

A commodity such as iron, corn or a diamond, is therefore, so far as it is a material thing, a use-value, something useful. This property of a commodity is independent of the amount of labour required to appropriate its useful qualities.

If we leave out of consideration the use-value of commodities, they have only one common property left, that of being the product of labour.

But it is not labour as some kind of metaphysical quality that gave commodities their value. Only **skilful** labour expended on the production of useful products or services is capable of producing value.

Some people might think that if the value of a commodity is determined by the quantity of labour spent upon it, the more idle and unskilful the labourer, the more valuable would the commodity be, because more time would be required for its production.

Skilled labour differs only in intensity from unskilled, and not in quality.

Skilled labour counts only as simple labour intensified, a given quantity of skilled being considered equal to a greater quantity of simple labour.

Necessary Labour Time

Marx, from this analysis of labour, went on to define the amount of labour required to produce a commodity, and consequently the value of commodities.

The labour time socially necessary is that required to produce an article under the normal conditions of production, and with the average degree of skill and intensity prevalent at the time.

The question now arises: if it is socially necessary labour time that determines the value of a commodity, what determines the value of labour itself?

The value of labour power is determined in the case of every other commodity by the labour time necessary for its production.

NEW WORKERS

This attempt to estimate the value of labour as a commodity went further than any of the theories of Smith, Ricardo or Malthus.

The value of labour power is the value of the means of subsistence necessary for the maintenance of the labourer.

The number and extent of his so-called necessary wants, and also the mode of satisfying them, are themselves the product of historical development and depend therefore to a great extent on the civilisation of a country.

Labour Power

In completing his description of the contractual nature of the free market, Marx distinguished between the labourer and what he sold – labour power. The labourer was technically free to sell his 'commodity' to the highest bidder, while the capitalist was under no obligation to provide for his welfare.

Accompanied by Mr Moneybags and by the possessor of labour power, we shall therefore take leave for a time of this noisy sphere, where everything takes place on the surface and in view of all men, and follow them into the hidden abode of production. Here we shall at last force the secret of profit-making.

Surplus Value

We will now see how, in spite of free contract between employer and employee, the capitalist can still extract surplus value from the worker without the coercive framework of feudalism or slavery.

WILL YOU WORK FOR A SHILLING A DAY WHICH WILL BUY YOU FIVE PIES. IF YOU'RE NOT SATISFIED WITH THAT, YOU CAN GO ELSEWHERE. O. K.?

A SHILLING A DAY — FIVE PIES? FINE!

The labourer, during one portion of the labour process, produces only the value of his labour-power, that is, the value of his means of subsistence. That proportion of the working day, then, during which this reproduction takes place, I call **necessary labour time**.

During the second period of the labour process, that in which the labour is no longer necessary labour, the workman, it is true, expends labour-power: but his labour being no longer necessary labour, he creates no value for himself. He creates surplus value.

The rate of surplus value is therefore an exact expression for the degree of exploitation of labour by capital, or of the labourer by the capitalist.

Marx then went on to outline the options open to the capitalist in order to increase his rate of surplus value.

WANT TO MAKE MORE PROFIT BY INCREASING YOUR SURPLUS VALUE?

Machinery: Relative Surplus

WHY NOT INTRODUCE MACHINERY?

Machinery is intended to cheapen commodities, and by shortening that proportion of the working day in which the labourer works for himself, to lengthen the other portion that he gives without an equivalent to the capitalists. In short, it is a means of creating surplus-value.

In so far as machinery dispenses with muscular power, it becomes a means of employing labourers of slight muscular strength, and whose bodily strength is incomplete, but whose limbs are all the more supple. The labour of women and children was, therefore, the first thing sought by the capitalists who used machinery.

Not only does it mean that I can hire weaker labour – but **cheaper** labour.

But many groups opposed this trend towards the replacement of labour by machines. With the introduction of mechanisation into the weaving industry, groups of displaced workers – the Luddites – smashed those machines.

Between 1800 and 1850 there were over a thousand such instances of machine wrecking.

But perhaps the biggest obstacle to this trend was the difficulties small capitalists experienced in getting the finance for such investment.

The exploitation of double the number of workmen demands not only a doubling of that part of constant capital which is invested in machinery and buildings, but also that part that is laid out on raw material and auxiliary substances.

Longer Hours — Absolute Surplus

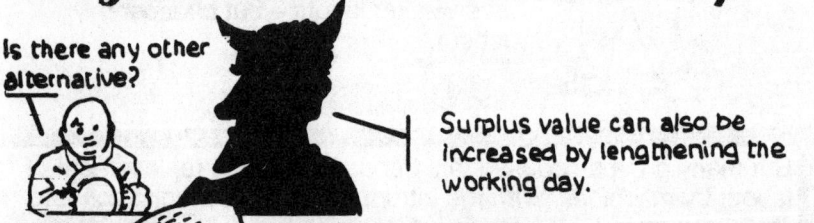

The lengthening of the working day, on the other hand, allows of production on an extended scale without any alteration in the amount of capital laid out on machinery and buildings. Not only is there, therefore, an increase in surplus value, but the outlay necessary to obtain it diminishes.

A long struggle had been waged in Parliament to secure a shorter working day, and in 1847 the Ten Hour Act finally limited to fifty hours per week the employment of 'young persons' and women of all ages.

Instead of lengthening the working day, some machinery was combined with new work methods, so that the pace of production could be increased.

Higher Productivity

This condensation of a greater mass of labour into a given period therefore counts for what really is a great quantity of labour.

The Industrial Reserve Army

This increase in productivity tended to increase the number of workers unemployed.

It is in the absolute interest of every capitalist to press a given quantity of labour out of a smaller rather than a greater number of labourers, if the cost is about the same.

As capitalist methods of production penetrated the countryside and destroyed cottage industry, the resulting unemployed were further augmented by the trend towards increased mechanisation.

WE WANT WORK! WORK, WORK!!

IF YOU WON'T PRODUCE, OTHERS WILL!

The overwork of the employed part of the working class swells the rank of the reserve, while conversely the greater pressure of the latter by its competition exerts on the former forces these to submit to overwork and subjugation under the dictates of capital.

The condemnation of one part of the working class to enforced idleness by the overwork of the other part, and the converse, becomes a means of enriching the individual capitalist, and at the same time accelerates the production of the industrial reserve army.

Wages were affected by the numbers of labourers in this industrial reserve army. When the economy was near full employment, the capitalist had no option but to pay higher wages in an attempt to win employees from his competitors. But when unemployment was high, the wage rate fell.

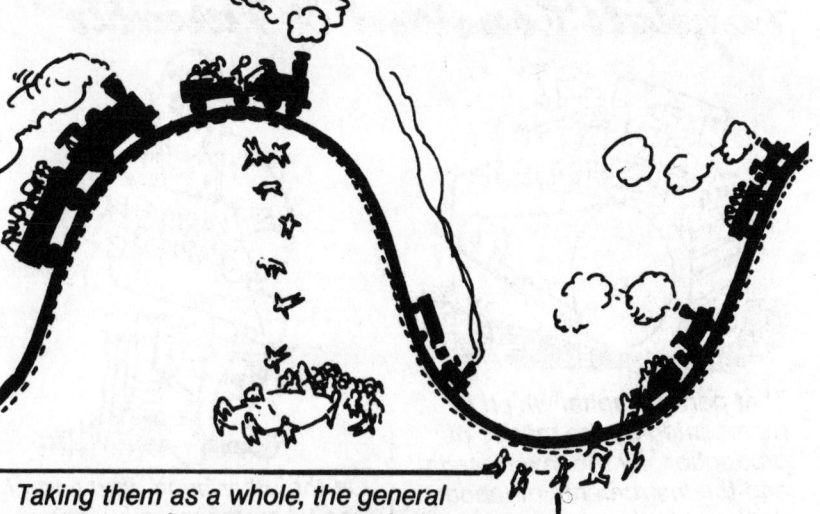

Taking them as a whole, the general movement of wages are exclusively regulated by the expansion and contraction of the industrial reserve army, and those again correspond to the periodic changes in the industrial cycle.

Having seen how the capitalist extracts surplus value from labour, we can now turn from the relation of the capitalist and the worker to the struggle between capitalists over their share of that surplus value.

To do this, we have to distinguish between constant and variable value.

Capital: Constant & Variable

FIXED CAPITAL

VARIABLE CAPITAL

That part of capital which is represented by the means of production, by the raw material and the instruments of labour, does not in the process of production undergo any quantitive alteration of value. I therefore call it the constant part of capital.

On the other hand, that part of capital represented by labour power does, in the process of production, undergo an alteration in value. I therefore call it the variable part of capital.

Organic Composition of Capital

The ratio of variable capital to constant capital (labour to machines) Marx termed the Organic Composition of Capital. The importance of this ratio can be seen when it is known that Marx denied that machinery could produce value itself, but was necessary in order to gain a temporary price advantage over competitors.

Machinery could produce no value itself since it was only a tool used by man; and the only value that it could pass on to the product that it assisted in making was the value that went into its own production. The more labour that went into the production of a machine, the more it could transfer, but not one iota more than that.

The first capitalist who introduces a new machine will gain a temporary advantage by being able to produce a given quantity of goods with less total labour for the same market price. He will then be able to sell them above their value. But as more capitalists introduce the same machine, prices fall, and capitalists are worse off than before because they have less labour to exploit.

IF THAT MACHINE CONTRIBUTES SO LITTLE TO PRODUCTION, YOU WON'T MIND IF I ROUGH IT UP A BIT.

OH YES I DO! THAT MACHINE REPRESENTS A CAPITAL INVESTMENT BY ME, AND IT INCREASES YOUR PRODUCTIVITY.

The Transformation Problem

Since wages, machinery and commodities have all been valued in labour terms, we now come to one of the thorniest problems Marx attempted to answer. What was the relation of prices to the labour embodied in commodities, and what was the relation of profit to surplus value?

I don't understand this stuff about 'Constant Capital', 'Variable Capital', 'Necessary Labour Time' and 'Surplus Value'...

My concern is with Profit, Wages and Capital. So if my accounting methods are totally different from yours, how can you claim to describe how Capitalism works?

Let us look at the prices and labour value problem historically. Primitive producers exchanged their goods at labour values, each being able to estimate the effort involved in the production of the other's commodity.

It took me a day to make this basket —I'll exchange it for your coat which it took you a day to make.

With the development of Mercantile trade the estimation of the labour involved in exotic products from distant lands became more difficult.

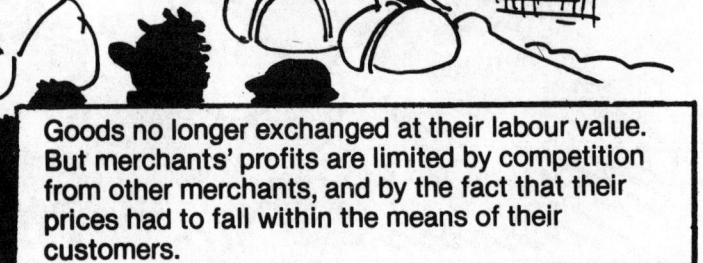

This took the goldsmiths of Siam two months to make.

Nobody here knows its true labour value so I've added a large profit margin for myself.

Goods no longer exchanged at their labour value. But merchants' profits are limited by competition from other merchants, and by the fact that their prices had to fall within the means of their customers.

With industrialisation, capitalists hired labour directly — instead of buying from independent producers — and reduced workers' standard of living by lowering wages. The surplus value they gained in this way gave them an advantage over their Mercantile competitors.

The extra profit gained by Capitalists allows them to sell their goods cheaper than their Mercantile competitors while still gaining average profit.

If in five branches of business, for example, the respective rate of profit is:

A 15% B 12% C 10% D 8% E 5%

Now folks, this is a model of how competition redistributes surplus value.

Then, the average rate is 10%; but, in order for this to exist in reality, capitalists A and B will have to give up 7% to D and E – more particularly, 2% to D and 5% to E – while C remains as it was.

A 15% B 12% C 10% D 8% E 5%

The capitalist class thus to a certain extent distributes the total surplus value so that it shares out evenly in accordance with the size of its capital, **instead of in accordance with the surplus values actually created by the capitals in the various branches of business.**

The number of firms reduced by the withdrawal of capital means I can increase my sales and prices. My profits will increase as those of A and B fall.

The larger profit – arising from the real surplus labour within a branch of production, the really created surplus value – is pushed down to the average by competition, and the deficit of surplus value in the other branch of business raised up to the average level by withdrawal of capitals from it, i.e. a favourable relation of supply and demand.

Total profits are now equal to total surplus value, but the price in a particular industry will no longer reflect the surplus value of that industry.

A B C D E

10% 10% 10% 10% 10%

A rise in the rate of profit here, a fall there, brings about such a proportion of supply to demand that the average profit in the various spheres of production becomes the same, so that values are converted into prices of production.

But that was far from the end of the question and much has been subsequently written on it. Here are just a few of the economists who commented on Marx's solution.

Bohn-Bawerk
Bortkiewitz
Sraffa
meek
Dimitriev

Accumulate to Survive

Having outlined the origin of the capitalist system, located to the sources of value, the surplus value of the capitalist and the competitive mechanism for the distribution of profits, what remains is to suggest the long-run dynamics of capitalism.

TIMES ARE TOUGH, BUT IF WE STICK TOGETHER WE'LL PULL THROUGH.

The development of capitalist production makes it constantly necessary to keep increasing the amount of capital laid out in a given industrial undertaking, and competition makes the immanent laws of capitalist production to be felt by each capitalist as external coercive laws.

Sorry... but it was either you or me!

It compels him to keep constantly extending his capital in order to preserve it, but extend it he cannot, except by means of progressive accumulation.

Capital Concentration

The battle of competition is fought by the cheapening of commodities. The cheapness of commodities depends, on the productiveness of labour, and again on the scale of production. Therefore, the larger capitalists can beat the smaller.

It will further be remembered that, with the development of the capitalist mode of production, there is an increase in the amount of individual capital necessary to carry out business in the normal conditions.

The smaller capitals, therefore, crowd into spheres of production where modern industry has only sporadically or incompletely got hold of. Here competition rages in direct proportion to the number and inverse proportion to the magnitudes of the antagonizing capitals.

It always ends in the ruin of many small capitalists, whose capitals pass into the hands of conquerors.

Falling Profits & Crisis

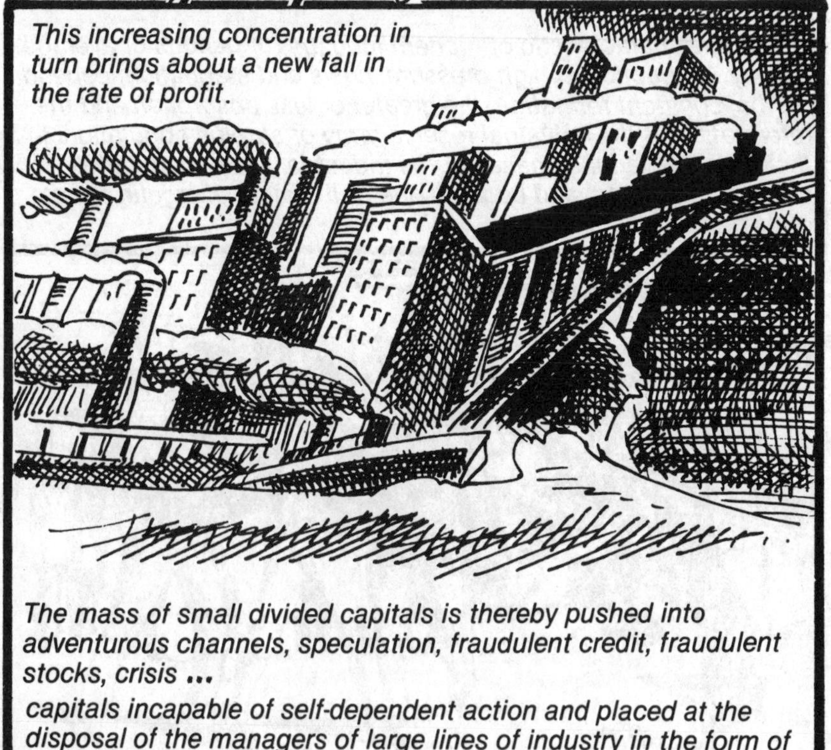

This increasing concentration in turn brings about a new fall in the rate of profit.

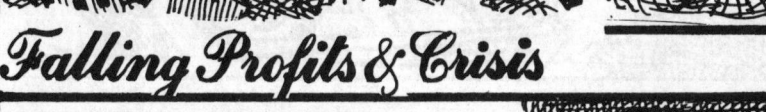

The mass of small divided capitals is thereby pushed into adventurous channels, speculation, fraudulent credit, fraudulent stocks, crisis ...

capitals incapable of self-dependent action and placed at the disposal of the managers of large lines of industry in the form of credit.

117

Business Cycles & Unemployment

As the economy moved from slump into rapidly increasing activity, it called upon the workers who had been shed by firms as they plunged downwards.

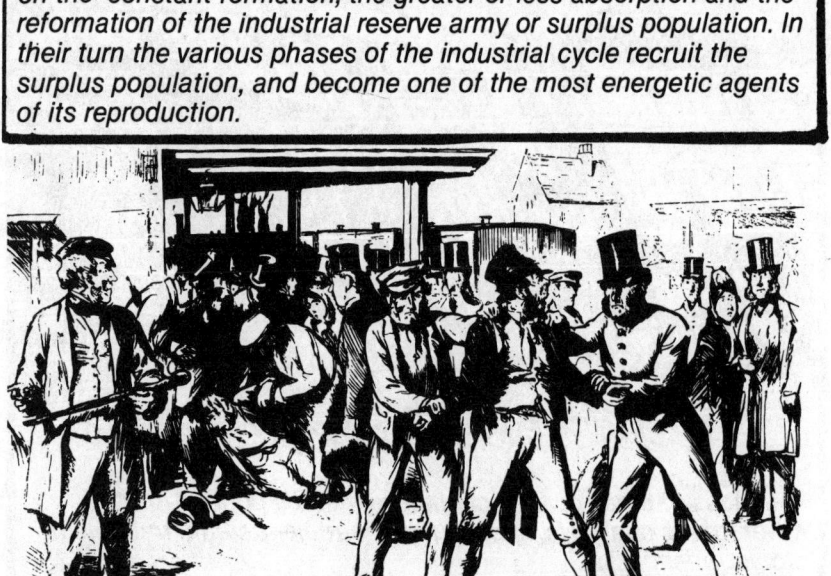

The course characteristic of modern industry, of periods of average activity, production at high pressure, crisis and stagnation, depend on the constant formation, the greater or less absorption and the reformation of the industrial reserve army or surplus population. In their turn the various phases of the industrial cycle recruit the surplus population, and become one of the most energetic agents of its reproduction.

HE WAS RECRUITING FOR THE INDUSTRIAL RESERVE ARMY.

118

And it is the polarisation of these two forces, capital and labour, which Marx predicted would bring about social revolution.

RUSSIA
CHINA
CUBA
CHILE
VIETNAM

Summing up

Marx's theory rested on two central arguments. The first was concerned with the mechanism through which surplus value was extracted from labour at the level of production. The second was an analysis of the way competition and accumulation affected the profits of capitalists over a long period.

Necessary labour is that required for producing the necessities required by the working class for their subsistence.

Necessary labour is bought by capitalists at the current wage rate which is determined by the numbers of unemployed – the industrial reserve army – who are competing with each other for work.

Wages are paid for given periods of production – the working day – which is determined by legislation in their interest, and the surplus produced over and above what is required by the workers is the property of the capitalist.

This surplus value can only be produced by labour and the capitalist is perpetually seeking for ways of increasing it.

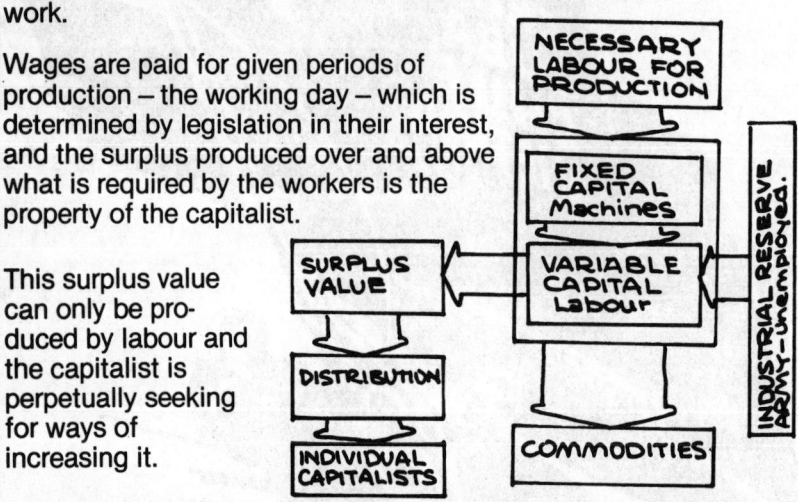

Capitalists are in competition with each other which equalises the rate of profit between them: if a particular capitalist finds a way of gaining more profit, other capitalists move into this sector of the market, thereby lowering his share of the profit.

This means that only total surplus value and total profit can be said to be equal, as the incessant movement of profit affects surplus value.

The long-term tendency is for some capitalists to expand at the expense of others and a centralisation and concentration of capital to occur in the hands of the more successful ones.

6

Alfred Marshall
1842 1924

And now for something completely different.

The 1870s saw the simultaneous development of the doctrine of Marginal Utility in Britain where W.S. Jevons (1835-82) published his **Theory of Political Economy**; in Austria with Carl Menger's **Grundsätze der Volkwirtschaftlehre**; and in Switzerland with Leon Walras' **Elements d'Economie Politique Pure**. Alfred Marshall also came to this idea independently during the same period but withheld publication until he had integrated it into his general economic theory in 1890.

MY IDEA!

Marginal Utility

The principle springs from the fact that people's appetites are satiable. The nearer they come to the point of satisfaction, the less they are willing to pay for further amounts.

When a boy picks blackberries for his own eating, the action of picking is probably itself pleasurable for a while; and for some time longer the pleasure of eating is more than enough to repay the trouble of picking.

But after he has eaten a good deal, the desire for more diminishes; while the task of picking begins to cause weariness, which may indeed be a feeling of monotony rather than fatigue.

Equilibrium is reached when at last his eagerness to play and his disinclination for the work of picking counterbalance the desire for eating. The satisfaction he can get from picking fruit is at its **maximum**.

Put into general economic terms...

UTILITY IS TAKEN TO BE A CORRELATIVE OF DESIRE OR WANT.

There is an endless variety of wants, but there is a limit to each separate want. This familiar and fundamental tendency of human nature may be stated in the law of satiable wants or diminishing utility. The total utility of a thing to anyone increases with every increase in his stock of it, but not as fast as his stock increases.

That part of a thing which he is only just induced to purchase may be called his marginal purchase because he is at the margin of doubt whether it is worth his while to incur the outlay required to obtain it.

And the utility of his marginal purchase may be called the marginal utility of the thing to him.

Marginal Demand Price

This psychological tendency can then be converted quite simply into money terms, and this by-passed the problem of value that Ricardo and Marx had made into such a controversial issue.

The larger the amount of a thing that a person has, the less, other things being equal, will be the price which he will pay for a little more of it; in other words, his marginal demand price for it diminishes.

BUT WON'T THIS DIFFER FROM PERSON TO PERSON, DEPENDING ON THEIR PREFERENCE AND THE AMOUNT OF MONEY THEY HAVE?

Yes, a greater utility will be required to induce him to buy a thing if he is poor than if he is rich.

BUT IF YOU ADMIT THAT THE MARGINAL UTILITY OF A POUND IS GREATER FOR A POOR MAN THAN FOR A RICH MAN, WOULDN'T SOCIETY AS A WHOLE GAIN BY REDISTRIBUTING WEALTH FROM THE RICH TO THE POOR?

Utility Maximising

HERE'S MY WAGES, NOT ENOUGH TO BUY ALL I WANT. SO HOW SHALL I SPEND IT BEST?

... DISTRIBUTE YOUR PURCHASING POWER SO THAT THE MARGINAL UTILITY ON EACH GOOD WILL BE EQUAL. THAT WAY YOU'LL GET THE MAXIMUM UTILITY FROM YOUR WAGES.

Supply & Demand

The general theory of the equilibrium of demand and supply is a fundamental idea running through the frames of all the various parts of the central problem of distribution and exchange.

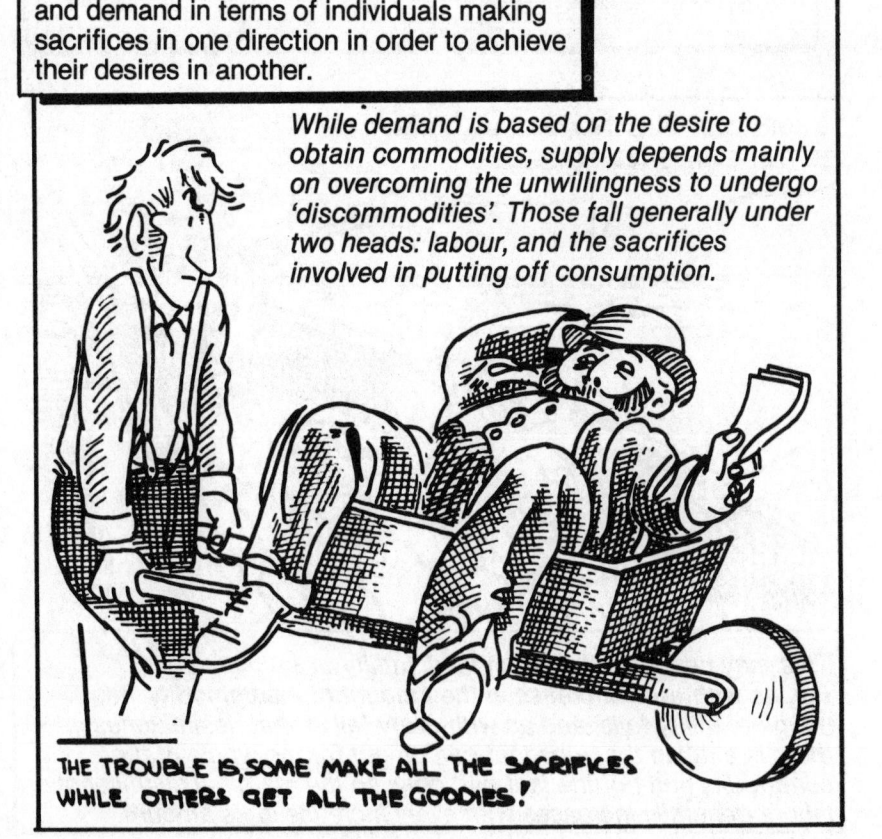

Marshall saw this tension between supply and demand in terms of individuals making sacrifices in one direction in order to achieve their desires in another.

While demand is based on the desire to obtain commodities, supply depends mainly on overcoming the unwillingness to undergo 'discommodities'. Those fall generally under two heads: labour, and the sacrifices involved in putting off consumption.

THE TROUBLE IS, SOME MAKE ALL THE SACRIFICES WHILE OTHERS GET ALL THE GOODIES!

Marginal Disutility of Labour

Whatever **disutilities** others have to forego, the labourer in the pursuit of his desire for wages has to endure physical effort which intensifies with every extra hour.

I SUPPOSE HIS **MARGINAL DISUTILITY** IS THE SAME AS OURS!!

This may be called the marginal disutility of labour.
For, as with every increase in the amount of a commodity, its marginal utility falls; and as with every fall in that desirableness, there is a fall in the price that can be got for the whole of the commodity and not the last part only; so the marginal disutility of labour generally increases with every increase in its amount.

Wages Equal Marginal Cost

But if the increasing disutility of work has to be compensated for by ever higher wages, what point will employers increase wages up to before they decide it is not worth their while to pay more?

A question constantly in the mind of the careful businessman is whether he has the right number of men for his work. Some express trains have only one guard; and when traffic is heavy they may lose a few minutes which could have been saved by a second guard.

…and therefore the alert manager is constantly weighing the net product in saving of time and annoyance to passengers, that will accrue from the aid of a second guard on an important train, and considering if it will be worth the cost.

The wages of an extra guard would be £1 a week. Could I get the extra revenue, or make a saving to that extent, over the course of a year which would cover the cost of his wage?

THE LAST TIME, DO YOU HEAR ME? THE LAST TIME!

So now we know the kind of pressures behind the employer's demand for labour, as well as the motives influencing the supply of labour. At the point where these two forces balance, we have the actual quantity of labour provided, as well as the going wage rate.

Waiting & Interest

If labour suffers the disutility of labour in the form of physical pain, what about the other classes that contribute to production, like the lenders of capital and the industrialists? Marshall's contribution was to reject the previous terminology.

IT PAINS ME TO LEND YOU THIS MONEY — HOW'S THAT?

NO, NO — TRY SAYING, I ABSTAIN FROM SPENDING NOW, SO I CAN INVEST— AND LOOK PAINED.

Karl Marx and his followers have found much amusement in contemplating the accumulation of wealth which results from the abstinence of Baron Rothschild, which they contrast with the extravagance of a labourer who feeds a family of seven on seven shillings a week; and who, living up to his full income, practises no economic abstinence at all.

Since, however, the term is liable to be misunderstood, we may with advantage avoid its use, and say that the accumulation of wealth is generally the result of a postponement of enjoyment, or of **waiting** *for it.*

In order to relieve those ever-increasing discomforts in the minds of those contributing to production, there had to be a corresponding increase in their compensation. Higher wages are necessary to overcome the fatigue of work, and higher interest rates are necessary to compensate investors for postponing their present consumption.

INTEREST RATES WOULD HAVE TO BE 3% HIGHER BEFORE I'D CONSIDER POSTPONING MY PRESENT ENJOYMENT AND INVEST MY MONEY INSTEAD

ANOTHER THREE HOURS AND I'LL BE ON TIME AND A HALF.

Supply Price

Marshall then brought those various factors together under a single heading.

Now we have to take account of the fact that the production of a commodity generally requires many different kinds of labour and the use of capital in many forms. The exertions of all the different kinds of labour that are directly or indirectly involved in making it; together with the abstinences or rather the waitings required for saving the capital used in making it. All those efforts and sacrifices together may be called the real cost of the production of a commodity.

The sums of money that have to be paid for those efforts and sacrifices will be called either its money cost of production, or, for shortness, its expenses of production; they are the prices which have to be paid in order to call forth an adequate supply of efforts and waitings that are required for making it; or, in other words, they are its **supply price**.

Price

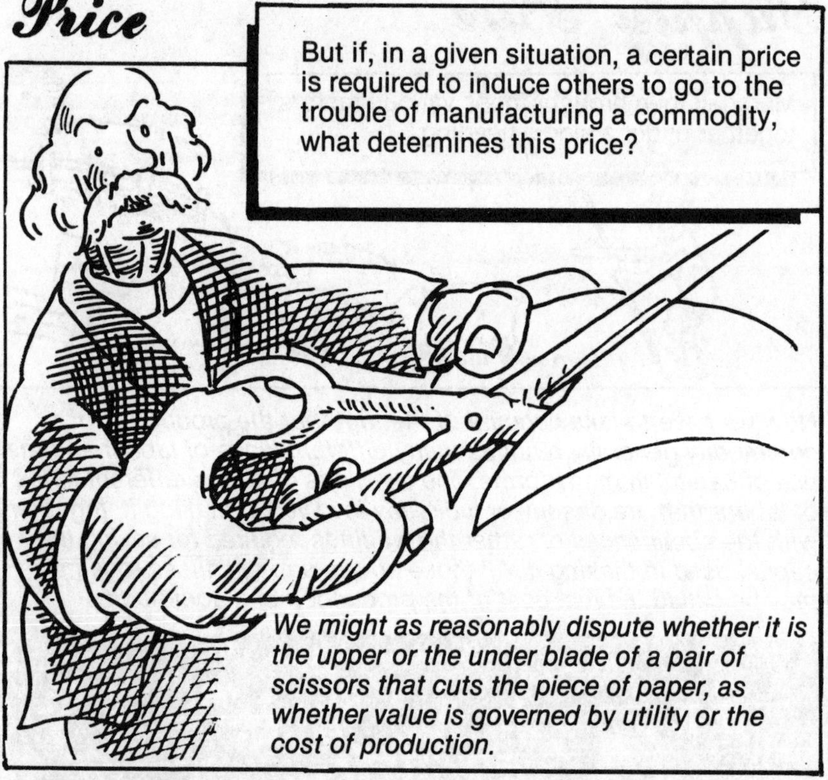

But if, in a given situation, a certain price is required to induce others to go to the trouble of manufacturing a commodity, what determines this price?

We might as reasonably dispute whether it is the upper or the under blade of a pair of scissors that cuts the piece of paper, as whether value is governed by utility or the cost of production.

The Representative Firm

We now have the basic determinants of price: the utility gained from consumption, and disutility of labour and **waiting** for interest. What remains to be shown is how this trade-off expresses itself through the institutions and operation of the market.

The consumer, the worker, the capitalist and the investor all meet in the primary institution of the capitalist economy – the firm.

Marshall invented the representative firm which allowed him to generalise about the behaviour of firms in the market.

WHAT SORT OF 'FIRM'? NOT A NEW PRODUCER JUST STRUGGLING INTO BUSINESS WITH LITTLE OR NO PROFIT.

NOT AN OLD ONE WHICH HAS PUT TOGETHER A VAST BUSINESS.

OUR FIRM IS THE <u>AVERAGE</u> ONE.

Economies of Scale

Although Marshall chose this medium-size firm as representative for the economy, he was well aware of a tendency which rendered any model based on such a firm highly artificial.   Large firms, for instance, can produce goods cheaper than small firms: every increase in the size of the plant of a firm gives increasing returns in output, and this advantage of size is known as an economy of scale.

In fact when the production of a commodity conforms to the law of increasing return in such a way as to give a very great advantage to large producers, it is apt to fall almost entirely into the hands of a few large firms; and then the normal marginal supply cannot be isolated on the plan just referred to, because the plan assumes a great many competitors with businesses of all sizes.

BOOM

THIS IS MONOPOLY— WHICH DISTORTS THE NORMAL LEVEL OF PRICE.

Principle of Substitution

In spite of this severe flaw in the competitive model, Marshall pressed ahead. As he had depicted the motivation of individual consumption as utility, he identified the motivation of the business firm as being profit-maximising. And in order to ensure this profit, firms continually adjusted production and inputs in such a way as to ensure that they are produced by the least expensive methods.

At the beginning of his undertaking, and at every successive stage, the alert business man strives to modify his arrangements so as to obtain better results with a given expenditure, or equal results with less expenditure.

In other words, he ceaselessly applies the principle of substitution, with the purpose of increasing his profits; and, in so doing, he seldom fails to increase the total efficiency of work, the total power over nature which man derives from organisation and knowledge.

The application of this principle extends over almost every area of economic enquiry.

Market Period

The enterprising capitalist ensures the maximum profit by substituting the more efficient factors for the less. And the market price dictated by the utility preferences of the consumers provides the signal for him to adjust his production so that supplies will satisfy the demand. But some time is required for this adjustment to occur. Marshall outlines the stages through which this happens.

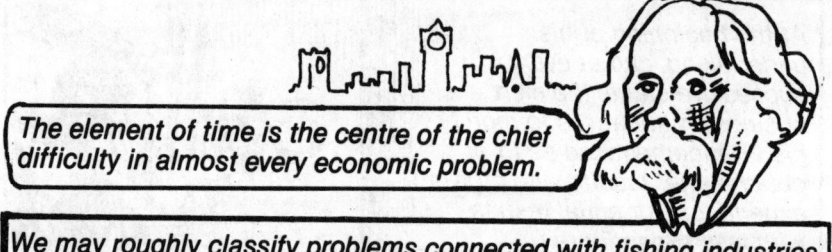

The element of time is the centre of the chief difficulty in almost every economic problem.

We may roughly classify problems connected with fishing industries as those which are affected by very quick changes, such as the uncertainties of the weather.

The changes in the general economic conditions around us are quick: but they are not quick enough to affect perceptually the short period normal levels about which the price fluctuates from day to day: and may be neglected during the study of such fluctuations.

Short Period

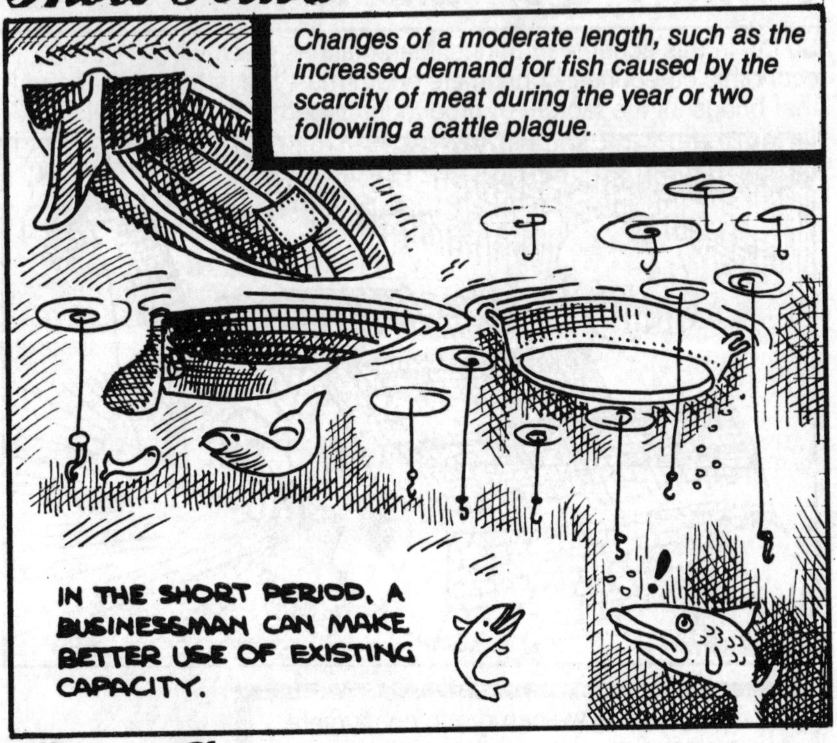

Changes of a moderate length, such as the increased demand for fish caused by the scarcity of meat during the year or two following a cattle plague.

IN THE SHORT PERIOD, A BUSINESSMAN CAN MAKE BETTER USE OF EXISTING CAPACITY.

Long Period

Or lastly, we may consider the great increase during a whole generation of the demand for fish

IN THE LONG TERM, I CAN INCREASE THE CAPACITY OF MY SHIPS AND BUILD NEW ONES.

Firms & Consumers

So far, in this scheme of things, Marshall has given us two new economic categories: consumers and firms – the latter being the unit that brings all the factors of production together in the market.

For convenience, we can group consumers into households who buy the goods produced by the firms out of the wages paid to them.

What about the economic classes of the Classics? Where have they gone?

Distribution

The Marginalist reformation of value and the introduction of consumers and firms as the prime economic units replaced the Classical division of wealth between landlords, capitalists and labour. With this new terminology, political economy was replaced by economics.

WELL, WHAT HAPPENED TO RENT, WAGES AND PROFIT, IF WE'RE NOT SPEAKING ABOUT LANDLORDS, CAPITALISTS AND LABOUR?

OH, WE'VE STILL GOT THEM. IN MODERN TIMES, RENT ISN'T JUST A RETURN ON FARMLAND, BUT IT COVERS OTHER FACTORS OF PRODUCTION, ESPECIALLY THE VALUE OF URBAN SITES.

AND WE NO LONGER RESERVE WAGES TO LABOUR. THE RETURNS TO MANAGEMENT FOR THEIR SKILLS IS NOW TERMED WAGES AS WELL.

Summing up

The alternative to the Classical system in the Anglo-Saxon world was provided by Marshall's **Principles**. It formed the basis of modern economics with its concepts of supply and demand, and its emphasis on the individual's perception of his utility.

The forces of supply and demand are what determine the quantity of goods offered and the price that will clear the market.

The supply side is determined by firms in competition with each other attempting to maximise profits.

The demand side is made up of consumers deciding how to allocate their incomes in such a way as to maximise their utility. Say's law still ensures that there is no general glut of goods supplied for which there is no demand.

If there is an over-supply of any particular product, its price will fall, the manufacturer will stop production, labour will be laid off, which in turn will contribute to lowering wages, and firms in other industries will find it more attractive to hire workers to expand their lines of production.

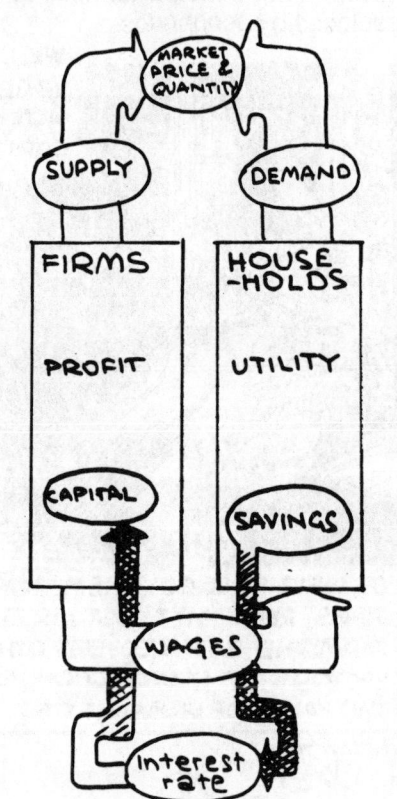

Marshall's picture of the economy as an aggregation of the actions of individuals and firms ignored the way social groups and classes acted in unison to influence the market – something Adam Smith constantly stressed. The inadaquacy of his picture of a self-regulatory economy where individuals and firms were rewarded according to their contributions became painfully clear in the slumps of the 1930s.

7

John Maynard Keynes
1883 1946

MARSHALL IS RIGHT, IF THE SYSTEM IS IN EQUILIBRIUM —BUT THAT'S ONLY ONE POSSIBILITY!

Marshall and the Marginal School switched the emphasis of economics from the production of wealth to its consumption. But they still maintained the Classical commitment to a rationalist system where all the factors and influences can be calculated.

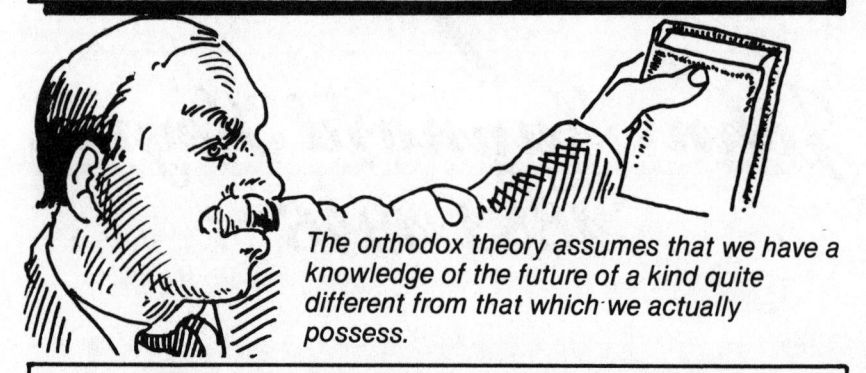

The orthodox theory assumes that we have a knowledge of the future of a kind quite different from that which we actually possess.

But the world of the 1930s, with the crash of the U.S. stock market, massive unemployment and general world collapse contrasted starkly with the ordered logic of the text books.

The practice of calmness and immobility, of certainty and security, suddenly breaks down. New fears and hopes will, without warning, take charge of human conduct. The forces of disillusion may suddenly impose a new conventional basis of valuation. All those pretty, polite techniques, made for the well-panelled board room and a nicely regulated market, are liable to collapse. At all times the vague fears and equally vague and unreasoned hopes are not really lulled, and lie only but a little way below the surface.

The Age of Uncertainty

Classical and Marginalist theories were confident only because they ignored the uncertainties in economic life and concentrated on the certainties.

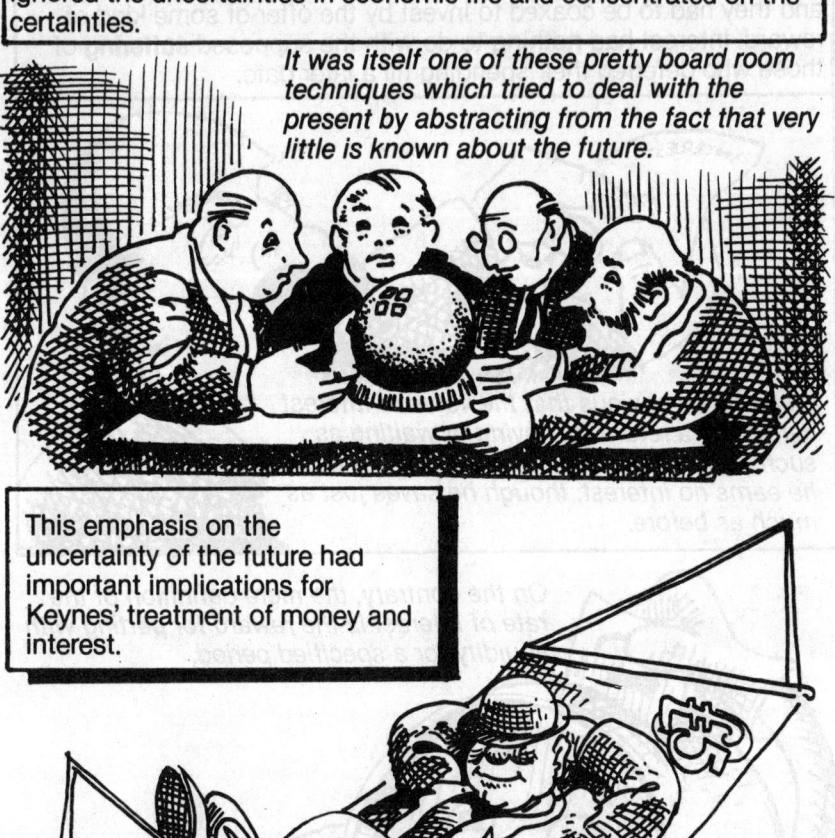

It was itself one of these pretty board room techniques which tried to deal with the present by abstracting from the fact that very little is known about the future.

This emphasis on the uncertainty of the future had important implications for Keynes' treatment of money and interest.

Partly on reasonable and partly on instinctive grounds our desire to hold money as a store of wealth is a barometer of the degree of our distrust of our own calculations and conventions concerning the future. The possession of money lulls our disquietude; the premium which we require to make us part with money is a measure of the degree of our disquietude.

Liquidity Preference

This disquietude about the future became the basis of Keynes' theory of interest rates. People held money out of fear for the future and they had to be coaxed to invest by the offer of some kind of reward. Interest had nothing to do with the supposed **suffering** of those who deferred their spending till a later date.

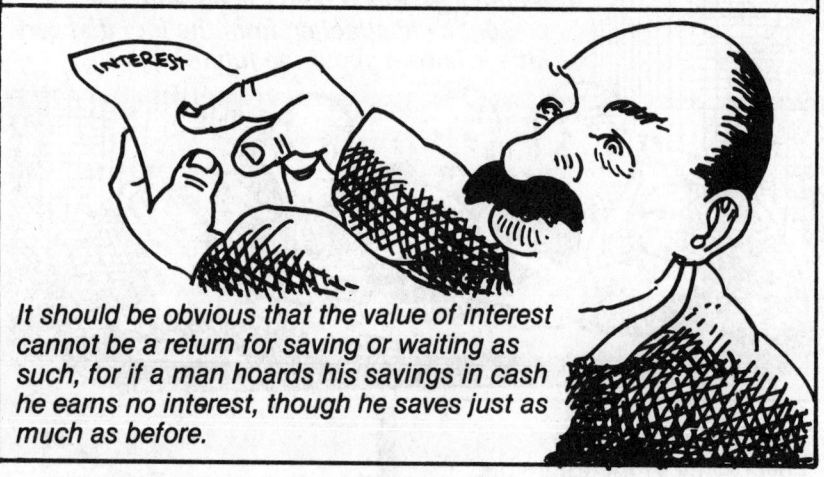

It should be obvious that the value of interest cannot be a return for saving or waiting as such, for if a man hoards his savings in cash he earns no interest, though he saves just as much as before.

On the contrary, the mere definition of the rate of interest is the reward for parting with liquidity for a specified period.

The fears and hopes that affected the demand for money – or the state of liquidity preference, as Keynes called it – countered the tendency to hoard, affected not the price level but the rate of interest.

How, then, was the rate of interest affected by liquidity preference? How does the rate of interest affect the total stock of cash held in the country?

It is the price which equilibrates the desire to hold wealth in the form of cash with the available quantity of cash.

Which implied that if the rate of interest was lower, i.e. if the reward for parting with cash had diminished, the aggregate amount of cash which the public would wish to hold would exceed the available supply.

And that if the rate of interest were raised, there would be a surplus of cash which no-one would be willing to hold.

The Stock of Money

This interplay between the preference of the public for holding cash and the existing stock of money controlled by the government determines the rate of interest. Put another way, the subjective factor is the stock of money circulating at any given time.

I DON'T FEEL HOPEFUL ABOUT THE FUTURE SO I'D LIKE TO PUT MY MONEY IN YOUR BANK

BANK RATES

THAT'S THE TENTH PESSIMIST TODAY, AND HALF THE EXISTING STOCK OF MONEY IN THE COUNTRY HAS BEEN BANKED

WELL, PRINT MORE MONEY. THAT WILL INCREASE THE AMOUNT IN CIRCULATION AND **REDUCE** THE VALUE OF HIS SAVING.

Hoarding

If the rate of return on investments is not sufficient to attract investors, they can either put their money into securities at the going rate of interest, or some may choose to hoard it and gain no returns at all. This last possibility is a refutation of the pre-Keynesian view that savings or current spending on consumption were the only rational possibilities.

WHAT ARE YOU PUTTING YOUR MONEY IN THE MATTRESS FOR? YOU'RE RUINING MY NICE ECONOMIC THEORY!

Assets & the Rate of Interest

Once the wealth-holder has decided to invest rather than hoard, he has two alternatives. He can lend his funds at current interest rates to those who wish to buy capital assets, or he can buy such assets directly himself.

LET'S LOOK AT BONDS, ONE FORM OF CAPITAL ASSETS. WATCH HOW **INTEREST** AND BOND **PRICES** ARE INVERSELY RELATED.

THIS BOND'S WORTH £100 AND YIELDS AN ANNUAL INCOME, £5 OR AN INTEREST RATE OF 5%.

O.K. I WANT 5%. HERE'S MY £100.

Later...

Big DEMAND FOR BONDS... PEOPLE THINK THERE'S A BOOM COMING. BUT I'M NOT SO SURE. I'LL SELL WHILE PRICES ARE HIGH.

I believe there's a boom coming. Since your bond yields £5% yearly, I'll give you £125 for it.

But £5 per year on £125 is only 4% interest per annum. So you can see that a rise in the price of bonds means a fall in the rate of interest and vice-versa.

Speculators

Let us now look at the behaviour of that strategic group of people in the economy who buy and sell these assets on the stock market – the speculators. They divide their wealth between cash and securities and gamble on the uncertainties about the future and the fluctuations in the market.

THINGS ARE LOOKING GOOD FOR THE FUTURE. SO I'LL PUT ALL MY CASH INTO ASSETS WHICH I CAN SELL WHEN PRICES RISE (BULLISH BEHAVIOUR)

THINGS ARE GETTING WORSE. ASSETS WILL FALL IN PRICE. I'M SELLING WHAT I HAVE. (BEARISH BEHAVIOUR)

Since their actions are governed by what they **think** will happen, if enough of them believe that the market will go in a certain way, then that is the way it will in fact go.

interest rate

Bond prices

Because of what speculators **expect** about the future of interest rates, there is a modification in the state of interest rates **now**.

What fool said that things are going to be better?

Interest rate

Bond prices

Only when wealth-holders have distributed their wealth between cash and assets in just the way that they are satisfied with, is there no change in the rate of interest.

INTEREST RATE

Stock of money (objective)

Attitude toward holding money (subjective)

Now we have seen how the rate of interest is determined by the subjective beliefs of the speculators and the general public, and the objective factor of the existing stock of money.

151

You UNDERSTAND THE STOCK MARKET, AND you've SPECULATED quite A BiT YOURSELF. WHAT do YOU THINK OF SPECULATORS?

Speculators may do no harm as bubbles on a steady stream of enterprise. But the position is serious when enterprise becomes a bubble on the whirlpool of speculation. When the capital development of a country becomes a by-product of the activities of a casino, the job is likely to be ill done.

The Great Crash

One of the most dramatic examples of this casino effect was the Great Crash on the New York Stock Exchange of 1929. After a year of frenzied speculation, Wall Street crashed on October 29th and the value of stock plummeted eventually to settle at a sixth of 1929 prices.

Marginal Efficiency of Capital

So far we have concentrated on the behaviour of spectulators, but are real investors, the men who run factories, swayed by uncertainties too?

Yes, there are uncertainties here too. Let me explain the concept of the Marginal Efficiency of Capital (MEC for short) or how investors decide how much to invest.

The schedule of the marginal efficiency of capital is of fundamental importance because it is mainly through this factor (more than through the rate of interest) that the expectations of the future influence the present.

THIS STEEL MILL WILL COST YOU £100,000, BUT WILL MANUFACTURE 1,000 TONS A YEAR. THAT'S THE OBJECTIVE FACT.

I HOPE TO SELL 1,000 TONS A YEAR AT £100 A TON FOR TEN YEARS. THAT'S A SUBJECTIVE BELIEF... GULP!

£100,000

The relation between the prospective yield of a capital asset and its supply price or replacement cost, i.e. the relation between the prospective yield of one more unit of that type of capital and the costs of producing that unit, furnishes us with the marginal efficiency of capital of that type.

BUT THE RATE OF INTEREST IS HIGH AT PRESENT. I WOULD BE BETTER OFF TO CLOSE DOWN MY EXISTING MILL AND PUT MY MONEY IN THE BANK.

True. The interplay between these two factors, the rate of interest and the MEC, determines the amount of investment and it is interesting to note that both depend on attitudes towards future returns – or subjective factors.

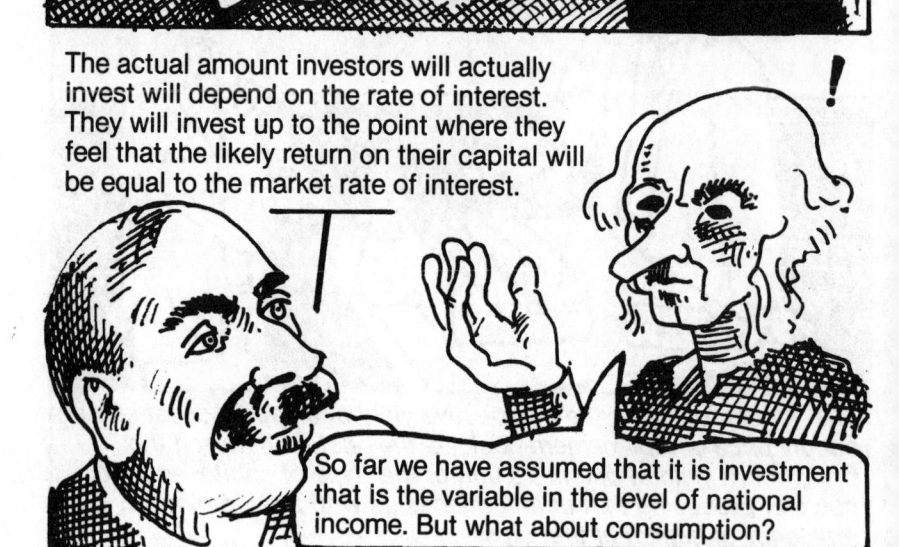

INVESTMENT

M.E.C. / Interest Rate

Price of Capital Assets (objective)

Existing Stock of Money (objective)

Expected Profits (subjective)

Attitudes towards holding Money (subjective)

The actual amount investors will actually invest will depend on the rate of interest. They will invest up to the point where they feel that the likely return on their capital will be equal to the market rate of interest.

So far we have assumed that it is investment that is the variable in the level of national income. But what about consumption?

Marginal Propensity to Consume

Consumption for Keynes was a function of income. Every consumer was faced with the decision, depending on the size of his income, of how much to spend and how much to save.

WE'VE SPENT MOST OF OUR INCOME ON OUR REQUIREMENTS, SO WE CAN SAVE THE REST.

SUPERMARKET

BANK

THE QUESTION IS—HOW MUCH THEY'LL SAVE. And if THEIR INCOME RISES, WILL THEY SAVE MORE, THE SAME, OR LESS?

In the main the prevailing psychological law seems to be that when aggregate income increases, consumption expenditure will also increase but to a somewhat lesser extent.

THE MORE WE EARN, THE MORE WE SPEND. BUT ALSO THE MORE WE'LL BE ABLE TO SAVE.

We now have the basic components of National Income levels and we can look at how Keynes combined these to give a dynamic picture of the economy.

The Level of National Income

The result of the Marginal Propensity to Consume (MPC) being stable meant that consumers do not bring about changes in the level of national income. So that means that only the investors can expand or contract the economy by their decisions.

CONSUMERS ARE CREATURES OF HABIT. AN INCREASED INCOME MEANS WE SPEND A BIT MORE AND SAVE A BIT MORE. BUT OUR EXTRA SAVING'S ALWAYS GREATER THAN OUR EXTRA SPENDING.

SO IT'S INVESTMENT WHICH DETERMINES THE LEVEL OF CONSUMPTION AND SAVINGS!

Our problem is that the people who save are a different set of people from those who invest. The actual savings that people make may not be identical to the actual investment made by investors.

The level of national income is what adjusts savings and investments. If households saved a portion of the circulating wealth and there was no investment, then after a time all of national income would escape through this leak.

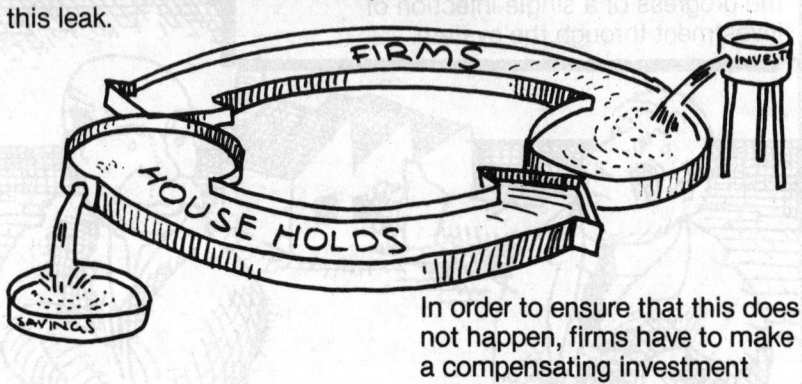

In order to ensure that this does not happen, firms have to make a compensating investment which replenishes the flow.

Marginal Propensity to Save

The Marginal Propensity to Save – MPS for short – is the reciprocal of the Marginal Propensity to Consume (MPC).

The MPS rises as income increases.

As we beome richer, we tend to save more and spend less of any extra income we receive.

The Multiplier

Let us now look at the way investment affects the level of national income and trace the progress of a single injection of investment through the system.

If we decide to invest, the extra money will pass from one sector of the community to another.

Yes, because you will hire more labour, and their extra wages increases sales from retailers, who'll also increase their stocks etc.

I want to invest this sum in new factory buildings.

The same sum of money would pass from one group to another ad infinitum if it weren't for the fact that people save a portion of their extra income. In that way, the extra income leaks out of the system.

Save ⅕; This is the proportion people are currently saving of any extra income they receive

SAVINGS

But in the course of passing from one group of consumers to another, the original sum invested has boosted National Income by many times its own value. If MPS is ⅕, then it will have boosted national income by a factor of five!

Definition: Savings = Investment

You'll remember that Keynes denied that the rate of interest was what brought an equality between what people wanted to save with what investors wanted to invest, and replaced this by the effect of investment on the level of national income.

Interest rate adjustments won't work, Marshall. You'll have to alter the income level.

Supposing that existing national income is £100m. and suppose that consumers spend £80m. and save £20 (an MPS of 1/5), investment must also equal £20m. if national income is not to fall. So what happens if investors decide to add an extra £10m. to the existing investment?

Won't a contradiction result between the £30m. investors now want to invest and the £20m. that savers want to save?

We want to invest £30m. but what do savers want to save?

We ONLY WANT TO SAVE £20m WHAT DO INVESTORS WANT TO INVEST...?

But if savers save less than investors want to invest, the difference – in this case £10 m – which is spent on goods will reduce inventories, defined by Keynes as investment, and the result is that savings still equals investment at £20m.

161

And what happens if investors want to invest **less** than savers?

We wanted to invest only £20m., but savers are saving £30m. So stocks to the value of £10m. have piled up in our warehouses. This way, <u>actual</u> savings always equal <u>actual</u> investment !!

AGGREGATE INVESTMENT

AGGREGATE SAVING

Theory of Employment

So it is through the adjustment of national income that savings and investment are brought into equality with each other.

Your theory, Marshall, which says the interest rate is the adjusting mechanism between investment and savings, doesn't explain the current position of the actual economy.

In the traditional view, the level of employment was related to an adjustable wage rate; if the numbers of unemployed increased, they would bid down wages and thereby stimulate enterprise.

I'LL WORK FOR HALF OF WHAT YOU'RE PAYING HIM!

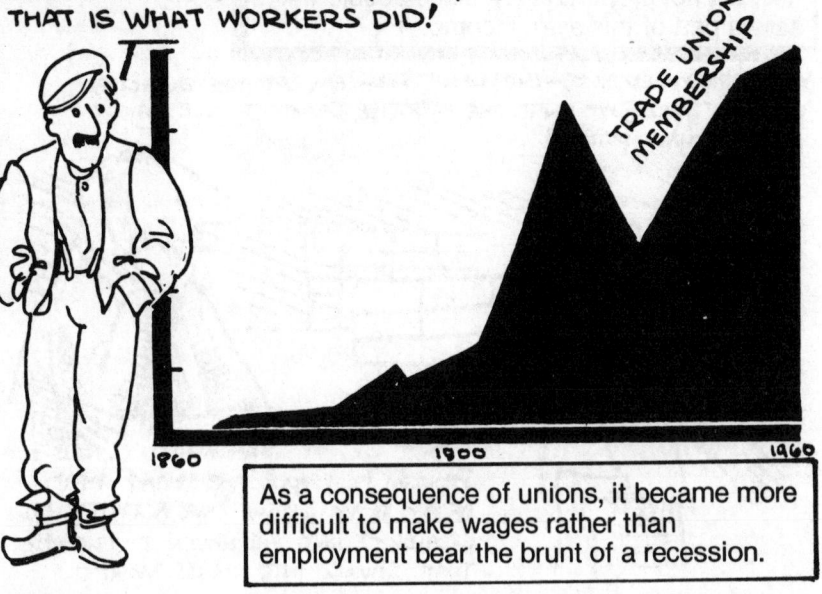

IF YOU WANT TO KEEP YOUR JOB AT YOUR PRESENT WAGE RATE, JOIN THE UNION, BROTHER!

Trade Unionism

AND AS A RESPONSE TO WAGE REDUCTION AND UNEMPLOYMENT, THAT IS WHAT WORKERS DID!

TRADE UNION MEMBERSHIP

1860 1900 1960

As a consequence of unions, it became more difficult to make wages rather than employment bear the brunt of a recession.

But Keynes gave another and more important set of reasons as to why the traditional arguments would not work. Let us suppose that employers had managed to bring about a reduction of the money wage rate.

THE GOVERNMENT'S INCOMES POLICY HAS BROUGHT WAGE RATES DOWN.

DAILY NEWS GOVERNMENT FIRM POLICY

GREAT! OUR COSTS ARE NOW DOWN: WE SHOULD BE ABLE TO PRODUCE AND SELL MORE GOODS.

Now we know that as economic activity increases, so will national income, and that the marginal propensity to consume will also rise, but not proportionally, since people will **save** a part of this extra income.

WE'VE PRODUCED MORE — BUT CAN'T SELL 'EM AT THE EXPECTED PRICES. THERE JUST ISN'T THE EFFECTIVE DEMAND. WE MAY HAVE TO LOWER PRICES!

PROBLEM IS, PEOPLE ARE SAVING PART OF THE EXTRA INCOME OUR ACTIVITY HAS CREATED — AND WE HAVEN'T TURNED THAT SAVING INTO INVESTMENT.

And why haven't investors invested that savings?

THE MARGINAL EFFICIENCY OF CAPITAL (THE RETURNS EXPECTED ON INVESTMENT) COMPARED TO THE RATE OF INTEREST I MUST PAY TO BORROW THOSE SAVINGS, ISN'T FAVOURABLE, IN MY OPINION...

For if entrepreneurs offer employment on a scale which, if they could sell their output at the expected price, would provide the public with income out of which they would save more than the amount of current investment, entrepreneurs are bound to make a loss equal to the difference;

...and this will be the case absolutely irrespective of the level of money wages.

Social Policy

So savings and investment will come into equilibrium, but not at the level of national income required to produce full employment.

What could government do to remedy this? Keynes had originally believed that it could be done through the adjustment of the interest rate by the central bank, but later rejected this strategy.

I am now somewhat sceptical of a merely monetary policy directed towards influencing the rate of interest.

I expect to see the state... taking an ever greater responsibility for directly organising investment; since it seems likely that the fluctuations in the market estimation of the marginal efficiency of capital... will be too great to be offset by any practicable changes in the rate of interest.

If the treasury were to fill up old bottles with bank notes, bury them at suitable depths in disused coalmines which are then filled up to the surface with town rubbish, and leave it to private enterprise on the well-tried principles of laissez-faire to dig up the notes again ... then there need be no more unemployment, and, with the help of the repercussions, the real income of the community, and its capital wealth also, would probably become a good deal greater than it actually is.

It would indeed be more sensible to build houses and the like, but if there are political and practical difficulties in the way of this, the above would be better than doing nothing.

Summing up

Keynes attacked two doctrines held by Marshall and the Classical school. The first concerned the impossibility of over-production or gluts: the more businessmen spent on hiring labour and purchasing raw material for production, the greater would be the sum of money chasing the finished products that left their factories. The second doctrine he attacked was the notion that all unemployment was voluntary, workers having it within their power to gain employment by accepting lower wages.

Keynes centred his analysis on the behaviour of businessmen. They provide employment and incomes in the form of wages, interest on capital and rent; and they expect to sell their products at a price that will cover all their costs, including a normal profit.

The amount of employment they are willing to offer is just equal to the volume of sales they anticipate making, so the economy can be in equilibrium at any point between zero and full employment. General wage reduction would not stimulate more employment. A single employer might take on extra workers as a result of higher profits and lower wages, but if all workers were to take a cut in wages, it would simply reduce the aggregate demand for goods, and thereby bring the economy to an even lower equilibrium level of employment and activity.

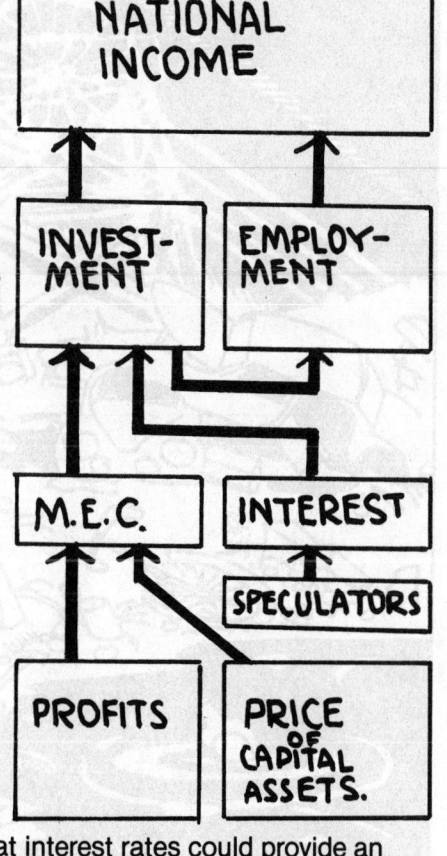

Keynes also rejected the idea that interest rates could provide an adjustment mechanism.

He looked instead to the actions of government to raise the level of national income through programmes of public works. Only the state had an overall and long term perspective of the economy, as well as the power to influence activity on a basis of general social advantage.

Glossary & Biographies

Smith

Adam Smith was born in Kirkcaldy, Scotland, in 1723, the posthumous son of a customs official. He was sent to Glasgow University in 1737 and afterwards to Balliol College, Oxford. In 1747 he went to Edinburgh where he lectured on literature for a year and became a friend of David Hume. In 1751 he gained a chair in Logic at Glasgow and in 1759 he brought out his **Theory of Moral Sentiments**. He left Glasgow to become travelling tutor to the young Duke of Buccleuch 1763-65, and accompanied him to France where he met Quesnay, Turgot and the other economists to Louis XV. From 1766 he lived with his mother at Kirkcaldy and worked on his **Wealth of Nations** which he published in 1776. The success of that work brought him to London where he joined the circle of Reynolds, Garrick and Johnson. He was appointed Commissioner of Customs in 1778 and returned to Edinburgh where he died in 1790.

Malthus

Thomas Malthus was born at Dorking in 1766. Educated at Jesus College, Cambridge, he was elected a Fellow in 1793, after studying Mathematics and Philosophy. He published his **Principles of Population** anonymously in 1798 in an attempt to refute the radical views held by his father's circle

Ricardo

David Ricardo was born in London in 1772, the son of a Jewish stockbroker. He had little formal education and joined his father's business at the age of fourteen. By the age of twenty he had already made a considerable fortune, and in 1793 he married a Miss Wilkinson and turned Christian. In 1799 his interest in Political Economy was awakened on reading Adam Smith. Encouraged by James Mill, John Stuart's father, he began to write on the subject. In 1809 he produced his pamphlet, **The High Price of Bullion as a Proof of the Depreciation of Bank Notes**. In 1817 his main work appeared, **Principles of Political Economy and Taxation**, which laid down the Classical foundations of economics. Already retired and living on his investments since he was forty, he entered Parliament in 1819 as a Radical M.P. for Portalington. He died at his country estate, Gatcombe Park, in 1823.

of friends. In 1803 he brought out a much enlarged version of the same work. In 1804 he was appointed the first professor of Political Economy at the East Indian College of Hailbury where he taught until his death in 1834. His other contributions to economics were contained in his **Principles** published in 1820.

Mill

John Stuart Mill, the eldest son of James Mill, was born in 1806, and was educated by his father. He began Greek at three, and before he was fourteen was well read in Greek, Latin, Mathematics and Literature, and had already begun the study of Logic and Political Economy. In 1823 he obtained a position with his father at the India Office, from which he retired as head of his department in 1853. In 1823-6 he was a member of the Utilitarian Society which met at Jeremy Bentham's house, but later considerably modified his views under the influence of the poets Coleridge and Wordsworth. He wrote extensively on Philosophy and his ideas on Economics are contained in his **Principles**. He was M.P. for Westminster 1865-68 and died in 1873.

Marshall

Alfred Marshall was born in 1842 the son of a cashier at the Bank of England. Like Malthus, he was a second wrangler in Mathematics at Cambridge and became a fellow of his college. When he was teaching mathematics at Cambridge he became interested in metaphysics, then psychology and finally settled on economics. In 1882 he moved to the chair of Political Economy at

Marx

Karl Marx was born in Trier, Germany, in 1818, studied philosophy at Bonn University and at the Hegelian Centre Berlin University, and took his doctorate at Jena. He became editor of **Rheinische Zeitung** in 1842 until it was supressed the following year and he fled to Paris. There he began his association with Engels and after a brief return to Germany he settled in England in 1849. There he began his investigations into Political Economy which were to take him the rest of his life and culminated in the massive **Capital**, the first volume of which was published in 1867. Three subsequent volumes of the work were published after his death in 1883. He published studies in sociology, politics, history and culture, all related to the materialist theory of history and the struggle between the classes, which has made his conception of society one of the central debating points of the Twentieth Century.

Bristol and lectured on the subject at Oxford. In 1885 he returned to Cambridge as professor of economics, a post he retained until his retirement in 1908. His most important works include **The Pure Theory of Foreign Trade** (1897) and **The Principle of Economics** (1890). He died in 1924.

Keynes

John Maynard Keynes was born in 1883, educated at Eton and Cambridge, where he graduated with a first in mathematics. He studied economics under Marshall and after a period as a civil servant he became lecturer in Economics at Kings College, Cambridge. In 1911 he became editor of the **Economic Journal**, and during the First World War he held a post in the Treasury, but resigned over the war reparations imposed on Germany. He published several important pamphlets on contemporary economic issues before he brought out his **Treatise on Money** in 1930. His major work, **The General Theory** appeared in 1936. During the Second World War he returned to the Treasury where he was responsible for negotiating the Lend-lease programme with the U.S. He took a leading part in the discussions at Bretton Woods in 1944 which led to the establishment of the International Monetary Fund. He died in 1946.

Books

There are several excellent histories of economic theory in print and others well worth seeking out in reference libraries. Among the best non-technical works available are Eric Roll's **A History of Economic Thought** (Faber & Faber) covering economic theory from ancient times to the present day; John Lekachman's very readable **History of Economic Ideas** (Harper International Student Reprint); and Maurice Dobb's **Theories of Value and Distribution Since Adam Smith** (Cambridge University Press).

For a more detailed account of the tributaries and currents of economic theory there is Joseph Schumpeter's monumental **History of Economic Analysis** published posthumously and uncompleted in 1954. And for a critical commentary using the tools of modern economic analysis there is Mark Blaug's **Economic Theory in Retrospective.**

Cheap editions of the works of the seven economists discussed are usually easy to obtain, and many reference libraries contain complete editions of their work.

Adam Smith **Wealth of Nations** (Everyman Library)

David Ricardo **The Principles of Political Economy and Taxation** (Everyman Library)

An Essay on the Influence of the Low Price of Corn on the Profits of Stock (Vol. iv Sraffa ed. **Works and Correspondence of David Ricardo** (Cambridge University Press) Malthus **An Essay on the Principle of Population** ed. Anthony Flew (Pelican Classic)

Principles of Political Economy (London 1820)

John Stuart Mill **The Principles of Political Economy**. ed. Donald Winch (Pelican Classic)

Karl Marx **Capital**. Vol. I, II, III, IV, **Theories of Surplus Value**, Part I, II, III (Foreign Languages Publishing House, Moscow)

Marx on Economics ed. Robert Freedman (Penguin)

Alfred Marshall **Principles of Economics** (Papermac)

John Maynard Keynes **The General Theory of Employment, Interest and Money** (Papermac)

Glossary & Index ▬▬

Capital The stock of goods, buildings etc. used in production which have been themselves produced. This stock of goods enhances the productivity of the other factors, **100, 107** land and labour, and usually entails some diversion of productive forces from consumer goods for their creation. The incentive for firms to invest in such capital goods is to keep up with, or overtake, their competitors. **116**

Consumption Function A concept formulated by Keynes to describe the relationship between total consumption expenditure in the economy, and total consumer's income. In his view, as income rose, consumption would also rise, but the rise in consumption would be less than the rise in income because some of the increases would be saved. **155**

Distribution Branch of economics devoted to how income from land, labour and capital is distributed between the different social classes **79, 84**. All the economists here, except Malthus, **65** thought a wider distribution of wealth throughout society was desirable; several thought the market mechanism was sufficient to achieve this end; **141** others that it required substantial government intervention, **85, 167** or that the market system should be replaced **119** by a planned economy to ensure that everyone gained an equitable portion of the wealth produced.

Effective Demand The mechanism which ensures that would-be purchasers have the necessary funds, **67, 69** or flow of income, **55** to buy the good produced.

Interest Regarded by Classical economists as the return to the capitalist for 'waiting' **131** or 'abstaining' **83** from immediately consuming his wealth. Keynesian theory related interest-rates to monetary phenomena such as the price of bonds **151** and the amount of money in the economy. **148**

Investment In everyday use the term usually means the purchase of assets which provides some form of monetary return, but strictly defined, investment means expenditure on capital goods. **17**

Labour One of the primary factors of production, comprising a variety of different productive services – skill, intellect, **79** physical effort. The Classical writers carefully distinguished between those types of labour which added value to a product **78, 95** and what they termed 'unproductive' **15** labour.

Law of Diminishing Returns The so-called 'law' relates to the observation that if one factor of production is increased by small, constant amounts and all quantities of other factors held constant, then after some point the resulting increases in output become less and less **62**. Strictly speaking, it is a hypothesis formulated within very restrictive assumptions, (fixed technology and homogeneous inputs), which remains yet to be proved.

Market. A market exists when buyers wish to purchase goods and services with money from sellers wishing to exchange these goods or services for money. **23** These forces of supply and demand determine the market price for goods; many buyers and few sellers mean high prices, and few buyers and many sellers mean low prices.

Market Period The time required for production to adjust to changed demand. **138** Both the extent of the market – the distance over which the producers are willing and able to come in order to trade **24** – and the amount of capital and labour which is required in the production of a particular good will affect the number of producers who respond to changed demand.

Marginal Analysis A marginal change is a very small addition or subtraction to the total quantity of some variable. Since much of economics is concerned with the maximising of a variety of variables:

consumers seeking to maximize utility; **126** firms seeking to maximise profits **129, 153** and governments seeking (it is assumed) to maximize social welfare, the measurement of small changes in these variables becomes central to much of economics.

Marginal Propensity to Consume (M.P.C.) The proportion of a small increase in income which will be devoted to increased consumption. **155**

Marginal Propensity to Save (M.P.S.) The proportion of a small increase in income which will be saved. Since saving has quite a different effect on National Income to consumption in Keynesian economic theory, it is important to measure the proportion saved and the proportion consumed of any extra increment to income. **157, 160**

Marginal Utility The marginal utility of any commodity is said to diminish with the consumption of successive units, the consumption of other commodities being held constant. **122** Many writers after Marshall found the notion of utility to be unsatisfactory: as a subjective quality, it proved impossible to measure and therefore useless in any comparison between different commodities.

Multiplier A term used by Keynes to denote the effect on National Income of a unit charge in some component of aggregate demand. If firms increase their rate of investment then we expect some growth in the level of national income; **158** the actual growth depends on how much of that income they pass on to other consumers in the form of extra purchases, and how much they decide to withhold, or save. The value of the multiplier is equal to the reciprocal of the fraction of income not passed on. **155**

Price The quantity of money which must be exchanged in order to secure one unit of goods or services. The 'natural price' or production cost of a commodity is what is just sufficient to cover the average cost of the materials, rent, labour and profit required for its production **133** – which may not be identical to the market price people are willing to pay. **30, 125**

Profit Various definitions of profit exist depending on accounting methods. Classical writers defined profit as the difference between the wages paid to labour and the value of labour's product. **41, 75** The Marginalist school defined it as the residual which accrues to the entrepreneur after all other costs have been met. **32** Competition between capitalists for maximum profit tends to create a uniform rate across all lines of production. **44, 46**

Rent The price paid per unit of time for the services of a durable good. The Classical school regarded rent as a monopoly on agricultural land alone; labour and capital might shift from one use to another, **33** but land never shifts to alternative uses: it is taken up when needed, not from other rent-paying uses but from nonpaying idleness. **40, 75**

Unemployment This can be the result of a variety of causes, such as seasonal unemployment among agricultural workers, structural unemployment as a result of long term changes in demand or technology, and 'frictional' unemployment where workers are out of work for a time between jobs. All the Classical economists noted the relationship between the numbers of unemployed ('the industrial reserve army') and wage-rates. **104, 118**

Value There have been several approaches to the theory of value. **43** The labour theory attempted to provide a measure independent of prices. **51, 54** Adam Smith defined it as the quantity of labour that went into the production of a commodity; **27, 95** but later changed it to the quantity of labour which a commodity might 'command' **29, 77** in a market exchange. Later writers identified the theory of value as identical to the theory of price, being simply how much an object will fetch in exchange. **134**

Wages For the Classical writers wages were fixed by capital: **97** wages could not be increased unless the capital destined to pay them was increased, **31, 39** and average wages were determined by the number of workers available to be paid out of a fixed wage fund. **76**

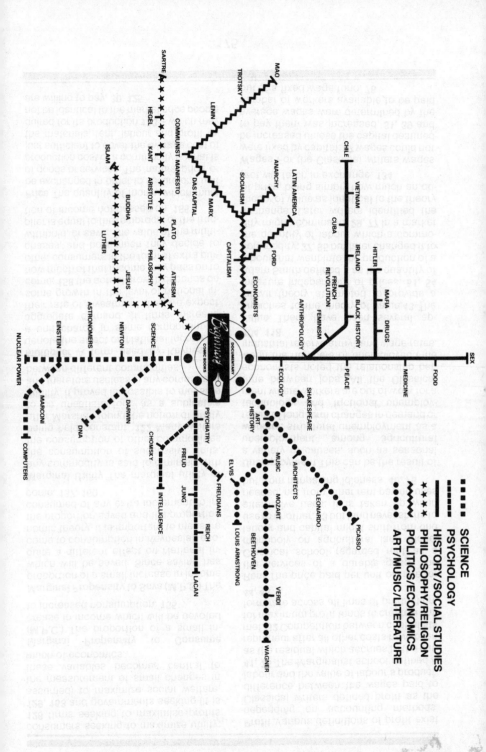